Questions in the Sand
Buddhist Questions and Answers
David Brazier

Previous books by David Brazier

A Guide to Psychodrama

Beyond Carl Rogers:
Towards a psychotherapy for the 21st century

Zen Therapy

The Feeling Buddha

The New Buddhism

Who Loves Dies Well

Her Mother's Eyes and Other Poems

Love and its Disappointment:
the meaning of life, therapy and art

Not Everything is Impermanent

Buddhism is a Religion

Questions in the Sand
Buddhist Questions and Answers

David Brazier

Woodsmoke Press

Questions in the Sand
978-0-9931317-2-1

Published by Woodsmoke Press 2017
Copyright © 2017 David Brazier

David Brazier asserts the moral right to be identified as the author of this work.
All rights reserved.

Cover photograph by Sanghamitra Adrian Thompson

Woodsmoke Press
Amida Mandala Buddhist Temple
Malvern
WR14 4AA

kaspa@woodsmokepress.com
www.woodsmokepress.com

To the Sangha

Preface

When I read the Suttas and Sutras which record the Buddha's teaching, one thing that stands out is how many teachings are given in response to questions. Someone appears before the Buddha with a spiritual dilemma, a burning question, a plea for their suffering to end, and the Buddha makes a compassionate response, guiding them towards insight and a growing faith in things beyond the selfish mind. Many of his responses come back to the same themes: karma, dependent origination, The Four Noble Truths and so on. There is a doctrinal thread that runs through the answers of the Buddha, and beyond that doctrinal thread there is a spirit of being in relationship to others and of living the spiritual life that shines through whatever the answer. What is this spirit? Compassion, wisdom, accepting each person that brings a question, loving each person that brings a question.

The same is true of the answers that Dharmavidya[*] gives in this volume. Many of his answers come back to the same teachings and themes: the importance of faith, the complexity and foolishness of human beings, the profound experience of a foolish being meeting the light of the Buddha. The answers

---

[*] Dharmavidya is the Buddhist name of David Brazier

show Dharmavidya's deep understanding of the teachings, his intelligent mind, his breadth of knowledge, but more importantly they show compassion and kindness to each questioner. The light of the dharma shines from every page.

I have been a disciple of Dharmavidya's for eleven years. He reflects the light of the Buddha like the dewdrop reflecting the moon that Dogen writes about in Genjokoan. The dewdrop is full of the moon, and yet it is not the moon, it retains its dewdrop nature, just as we retain our human nature. Dharmavidya reflects the perfect light, and retains his human nature. In this he embodies the great wisdom of Pureland Buddhism: whatever we are tangled up in, whatever our karmic state, the moon is always shining and all we have to do is turn towards it.

These are all questions that have been written to Dharmavidya over the years. Some of the questions here appear universal; questions that we will all recognise. Some appear to be more idiosyncratic; they seem to speak to just one person's koan. But one translation of the word koan is 'universal case', and however personal these questions seem, there is something we can learn from each of them.

As well as thanking Dharmavidya for his answers, I'd also like to thank those who asked the questions. Without you this book wouldn't be here.

'Questions in the Sand' was the title of the blog where these questions and answers were originally published. When I think of the title I imagine the tide washing over the beach and smoothing out the sand in which our heartfelt questions have been written. This image serves as a nice counterpoint to the care and attention Dharmavidya has given each question here.

On the one hand they are deeply important. On the other hand they are ephemeral and impermanent. It also brings to mind how each answer points us towards reality. The question is written in the sand, and the answer is the sea sweeping over it, and the birds and the sky and the sunshine.

Throughout my time putting this book together my gratitude for my teacher and for his teachers has been increasing and increasing. I have found a wealth of Dharma gems here, and I hope you are able to see them shining too.

Namo Amida Bu

Kaspalita Thompson

Contents

Preface	vii
Why Buddhism?	1
Metaphysics	4
Why Amidism?	8
Why Amida Shu?	10
Faith Beyond Despair	13
Buddhas Exist	16
Ritual and Message	19
The So-Called Marks or Signs of Being	22
Guilt	25
Faith and the Eightfold Path	29
What is Nembutsu?	33
The Power of Mantras	35
Amidist Nembutsu	38
Benefits of Nembutsu Practice	41
How Do We Proceed?	43
Mondo	46

Evil Beings in the Pureland	48
Nembutsu Practice and Mindfulness in Daily Life	51
When is the Pure Land?	53
Mother Buddha	57
Bombs, Victims and Persecutors	59
Self-Care	63
Trikaya	67
The Unborn	69
The Deathless	71
Was Buddha Self Power or Other Power?	73
Dukkha-Dukkha & More Dukkha	76
Buddha and Derrida	79
Secondary Faculties	81
Amida Pureland and Other Practices	84
Secretly Taking on the Sufferings of Others	86
Religion or Psychology	90
Obedience	93
Live with Wholeness of Heart	95
Duality & Nonduality	98
To Err is Human, and We Do Not Stop Being So	102
Mixing Practices — Cultivating Friendship	104
Many Right States of Mind	106
The Merit in Being a Hermit	108

How Is It to Be Alone?	111
The Happiness Trap	114
Does compassion start with oneself?	117
Attachment to the Guru	123
Thought, Word and Deed	126
Can Purity Survive an Impure Society?	129
How Can One Keep to Principles in a Corrupt World?	132
Does Equanimity Imply Incapacity to Make Judgements?	135
Problems with Ideas of Loss, Love and Attachment	137
Is Oneness the Goal of Practice?	141
Is Meditation Necessary?	147
Do Amida Buddhists Meditate?	151
What Can One Do When Spirituality Seems Unreal?	154
Delusion	157
Wavering Faith	159
Do Pureland Buddhists Practice Intercessory Prayer?	161
Metta	163
Personal Practice verses Relationship	165
No 'How to' in Nirvana	168
Experiencing Universal Love	170
Even Good People go to the Pure Land	173
Precepts or Not?	177

Practising while Sinning	179
What Happens When an Amidist Dies?	182
Other Lives	184
What is Buddha?	186
How Should I Regard Amida?	194
Adhisthana	200
Why do Buddhas Put Out Their Tongues?	204
Isn't Pureland More Like Christianity Than Like Buddhism Itself?	206
What is Meant by Saying: Good Ultimately Prevails?	210
Are Some People evil?	214
What Does The Amida Logo Mean?	216
A Few Questions on The Amida Shu Perspective	218
Sexism in Buddhism	223
Social Engagement	226
Do Social Engagement and Practice Conflict?	230
Socially Engaged Hermit?	234
Does Faith in The Future Imply Faith in This World?	236
Is The Buddha Portrayed in New Buddhism Academically Correct?	239
Natural Disasters	241
What is The Buddhist View of Romantic Love?	243
Phantasy and Transference	247

Can we be Enlightened Yet Still be Overwhelmed by Our Animal Nature?	251
Does Buddhism Offer Wholeness and Healing?	253
Anxiety	257
Addiction	260
Some Questions on Zen Therapy	264
Buddhism and Christianity	271
Buddha and God	281
Suicide	283
No Nature	286
For Love	290
Glossary	292

Why Buddhism?

Question: What is Buddhism and why be a Buddhist?

Short answer: It is one of the best commitments you can make in this life.

Longer answer: Buddhism is the spiritual tradition that derives from the teachings of the sage Shakyamuni Gotama who lived in India 2500 years ago. He, however, declared that the wisdom that he was spreading did not start with himself. He awakened to it and invites us to do likewise and put our trust in that perennial wisdom. Buddhism is, therefore, a path of awakening. To be a Buddhist, one has to have some faith in such awakening, yet it is actually a life of faith that one awakens to.

Let us look at this a different way. The disease of everyday life is the over-estimation of self. We all go around acting as if oneself is far more important than is objectively the case. This is just as much true if one considers oneself a victim as when one is self-confident and assertive. Everything we see, hear, encounter in any way, we distort by the powerful force of self-bias. Thus, Buddhist awakening has much to do with relinquishing self and its concomitant grasping, clinging, neediness, hidden agendas, and manipulation. However, if one seriously does this, then upon what is one going to base one's life? Generally people use the claims of the ego as their compass. If you throw that away, you enter an open field with many possibilities. It takes great faith to do that.

In fact, one has to replace the faith in ego with something and in Buddhism we replace it with "Taking Refuge in Buddha, Dharma and Sangha". All the rest of Buddhism is really a matter of exploring and unpacking what this means. What is Buddha? What is Dharma? What is Sangha? What is implied by relying upon them? What kinds of conduct, thought, view, concepts, effort, image and so on are entailed? Buddhism is a religion, which means that it has many dimensions — personal, cultural, spiritual, artistic, and so on. It has given rise to whole civilisations. It cannot be reduced to a single technique or idea. In fact, it implies a resistance to the kind of reductionism that is common in our modern culture. Buddhism is not just an "add on" — it implies a shift in the fundamental paradigm that rules one's life.

I became Buddhist because I had had spiritual experiences and was seeking an explanation. Read in that context, Buddhism made sense of things that were hard to make sense of by other approaches. Buddhism also offered a philosophy of peace, both personal and in the world. The world needs an approach that gives spiritual depth to life and spreads peace. Buddhism teaches generosity, gratitude, energy, patience, and a brand of wisdom that never ceases to push one further and further beyond one's current certainties. I have been involved in it for half a century now and it still challenges me. I'm a free thinker and Buddhism encourages my investigations. It provides me with useful tools for exploring the spiritual world and does not confine me in a straitjacket.

As Pureland Buddhists we have, in the Larger Pureland Sutra, a vista that gives meaning to life on a vast scale, a manifesto for a more perfect world both here and hereafter, and a simple practice that is suitable for anybody, that can be a medium for spiritual development and exploration and is as suitable for the most ordinary person as it is for the saint or hero — more so in fact. I don't know a better vehicle.

Metaphysics

Question: Is metaphysics necessary?

Short answer: You can't do without it, but mostly it remains invisible, embedded in people's taken for granted assumptions.

Longer answer: This type of question is generally rooted in the reductionist tendency of our culture, the desire to only allow concrete sense data to be considered "real". However, even that assertion is metaphysical. Metaphysics is the study of what we consider to be, or allow to count, as real, as well as of the basic rules and organising concepts by which we fundamentally structure our thought. We cannot function without such structure, but we can keep in mind that no such structure is final.

If we try to think deeply about life, existence, meaning, causes, consequences and all the other things that are of fundamental importance, then we cannot avoid operating according to one metaphysic or another. Not having one is not an option. It is a matter of choosing between them.

So how does one choose? There is no guaranteed method, no way to know for sure what is right. This is part of the reason that people are reluctant to look at it. You can't ever be certain. Furthermore, if you are wrong, then probably many other things that you have thought on the basis of your wrong assumptions are also going to become suspect.

Reflecting upon this question simply brings us up against our inevitable ignorance and limitation. We cannot see things with a God's eye view. On the other hand, we can look around us and see the lives of other people. The metaphysical perspective that a person holds will affect their life. We can make a judgement to some extent based upon such observation and this is often how people do make their decision, though often not consciously. They simply identify with some people and the fundamental attitude of those people then rubs off on them.

In Buddhism, therefore, one is likely to be attracted, firstly, either to a particular teacher, or a particular Sangha group. This is not a bad way to proceed. If you see good in those people, then having their basic attitudes rub off on you is not going to be a bad thing. As Buddha says, "Keep good company."

Perhaps, initially, you think that some of their ideas are strange and do not tally with what you have heard elsewhere. Perhaps you thought that people who think what these people think cannot be sane or kind or creative, yet, here they are! That may make one rethink.

The very activity of endlessly reconsidering the basics is valuable. Perhaps the first really important metaphysical proposition to hold onto is: We don't know that much. This will enable one to avoid becoming overly fixated on one's supposed certainties.

People who try to reject metaphysics often couple this in their mind with rejecting dogmatism. However, their own rejection is often rather dogmatic and there is no inherent reason why metaphysical propositions should be asserted more stridently than any others, except that they do, often, underpin much of the rest of what one believes.

In any case, dogma as such is not a bad thing so long as one holds onto it lightly. All it really means is "axiomatic". It is a dogma of Euclidian geometry that the shortest distance between two points is a straight line. Nowadays there exist non-Euclidian geometries that have other dogmas.

Thus, Buddhism teaches a "middle path". Some things one has to accept "dogmatically", but one has also to remember that this is provisional. Later one may change one's ideas. Thus the first step in Buddhism is to take refuge in the Three Jewels (Buddha, dharma and Sangha). As one goes on in the Buddhist path, one's appreciation of what this means will grow and develop and may change.

Buddhism is "dogmatic" in having some axioms, but it is not dogmatic in the sense of being narrow-minded and blinkered. The trouble really is to do with Western history. So many people have been persecuted or burnt at the stake for asserting the "wrong" ideas that we now feel over-sensitive about the whole issue, quite understandably. However, Buddhism is different. Of course, one will not have all the right answers straight off and one is not going to be persecuted in Buddhism for a difference of doctrine.

My suggestion, therefore, is to become relaxed about this question. Don't worry. All will become clear from time to time, and then it will get muddy again and then clear again and so on. Excluding the whole idea of metaphysics is what is most likely to make us narrow minded and to limit our exploration, so loosen up.

Most people have several metaphysical systems running simultaneously, not realising the inconsistencies that this brings into their thought – like a library in which several teams are at work each classifying the books on a different basis so that books that have been sorted on one system are being re-sorted on another and a lot of books are in stacks on the floor, not yet fully belonging to any particular category. Mostly our heads are a bit like that. The answer is not that of getting a perfect cataloguing system, but of becoming more relaxed about the whole business. It would be like that. We're human.

Why Amidism?

Question: What is special about Pureland Buddhism and devotion to Amida?

Short answer: A realistic view of persons, a generic spirituality and a simple practice.

Longer answer: Pureland Buddhism evolved from the Buddha's teachings to lay people. Most other forms of Buddhism are monastic traditions. Now monasticism is wonderful, but most people are not going to do that. When Shakyamuni died his relics were divided and stupas (small pagodas) were set up in many places, initially all over northern India. These became places of pilgrimage and worship. People came, circumambulated the stupa, made prayers and prostrations, gave offerings, and received the energy that emanated from the place associated with the great sage.

This was a simple, basic, generic form of spirituality. People could express their devotion in a practical way and receive help and teaching as well.

People had a sense that there was something very special about the Buddha and that that special quality did not die when the physical body died. In some sense Buddhas are eternal. Buddhism forbids too much speculation about what this means, exactly, but it is a palpable sense. Buddha himself had talked about Buddhas of past, present and future and there is, in Buddhism, a general sense of a vast spiritual realm of enlightened beings who can help us if we turn our hearts and minds to them.

So here there is faith, but also an acceptance of human limitation. There are many things we cannot know, but that is not a good reason to close our hearts and minds.

Thus, the basic attitude of Pureland, or Amidism, as it is also called, is that of recognising the bombu nature of the ordinary person — that we are limited, ignorant in many ways, vulnerable, prone to make mistakes and often ruled by wayward passions. We might try to overcome these but we shall not be completely successful. The important thing is to recognise the reality.

This therefore is Buddhism for ordinary beings and it therefore centres upon the Buddha of All Acceptance, Amida.

The sense is that Amida accepts us just as we are, so long as we turn toward him and the means of doing so is to call him. This calling is called nembutsu. The usual form of the nembutsu is "Namo Amida Bu". Namo means "I call upon" or "I take refuge in". The "Bu" is short for Buddha.

So Amidists are ordinary people who say "Namo Amida Bu" with some faith that by doing so they connect themselves with a source of spiritual grace that is vast, loving and redemptive. That is it, really.

Why Amida Shu?

Questions:
1. What led you to switch from Zen to Pureland?
2. How did you know you were ready to teach?
3. Why did you create Amida Shu as opposed to aligning with Jodo Shu?

Short answers:
1. Natural progression;
2. Acknowledgement by teachers plus existence of disciples;
3. Practicality.

Longer answers:

1: I trained in Zen with Kennett Roshi. She was definitely a "religious" Buddhist. She was completely out of sympathy with the secularising trend, had originally wanted to be an Episcopalian minister, deeply appreciated the transcendental and mystical aspect of Buddhism and taught Zen in terms of reliance upon the "Cosmic Buddha". She trained in Japan and the whole of Buddhism in Japan is influenced by other power. Tathagata in Japan is Nyorai, literally "he who comes to save us". To me, Pureland expresses what I learnt from her better than any other approach.

Of course there are also still recognisably Zen elements in my style and these continue in Amida Shu.

2: Kennett Roshi recognised that I had had kensho experience. Gisho Saiko Sensei asked me to bring Pureland to the West. Adachi Sensei senior told me to "be another Honen Shonin". I got the message. Furthermore, there were people wanting to practice with me. I did not feel terribly confident to begin with, but I did my best. Gradually, as the practice community has matured I have found my feet and together we have evolved something that seems to me rather wonderful in the form of a Sangha community where there is palpably great love, trust, faith, commitment and willingness. The Dalai Lama was once asked when you know somebody is a teacher and he said when there are genuine disciples. I am profoundly grateful to the people who have put their trust in me and I see my role as simply to ensure, as best I can, that they thrive spiritually.

3: Doctrinally it would be difficult to put much space between Amida Shu and Jodo Shu, or even Jodo Shin Shu. The differences between the two major Japanese brands of Pureland seem rather academic if you are not Japanese. Shinran, founder of Jodo Shin Shu, believed himself to be a true disciple of Honen, founder of Jodo Shu. Nonetheless, new schools emerge. In our case it was largely practical. Very few Western Buddhist denominations are still attached to Japan even if they started off that way. We did not even start like that. We evolved. It is much better for the spiritual health of our community that it be self-regulating, though we remain in good spiritual friendship with our Japanese fellow practitioners. The name Amida Shu came about through a conversation with the abbot of Anraku Ji temple in Japan, who started to refer to us by this term. We kept it. Organisational independence enables us to evolve more quickly and to incorporate aspects of Western culture as skilful means without changing the core message. It also means we can put the core message into Western language. So, it all works better this way.

Faith Beyond Despair

Question: I just read your essay on the first of the "12 Steps" in Running Tide number 33. In it you say, "In Pure Land Buddhism we admit that we do not have the power to enlighten ourselves. In this there is a kind of despair and a kind of faith."

I certainly know the despair; but, how does that engender faith?

Short answer: There is only room for faith in other power when we give up or despair of faith in self power.

Longer answer: Self power, jiriki, is the belief that one can achieve one's own salvation (however one conceives that) by one's own effort. All schools of Buddhism seek to demolish this kind of arrogance, but they go about the task in different ways. In some schools, such as Zen, the strategy is often that of having you try as hard as you possibly can until eventually you give up. That giving up is called kensho or satori if it is genuine. It is genuine when you know in your blood and bones that what you have been doing up to that point is futile. This is in imitation of Shakyamuni Buddha who, on awakening, realised that what he had been doing up to that point had been "vain, ignoble and useless."

In other schools, such as some branches of Theravada, the method is to deconstruct the idea of self, partly analytically and partly by such experiential exercises as the charnel ground meditations in which one observes and visualises the stages of decay of the body after death.

Then again, in yet other schools, notably the Pureland ones, the emphasis is more upon making a choice and turning to the Buddhas from a position of acknowledging one's inherent incapacity. This is very similar to the 12 step method.

> *"Shakyamuni Buddha... ...in his great compassion, provided something for everybody."*

Obviously, different approaches tend to suit different personalities, which is to say, different initial koans. However all of these and other methods derive directly from the teachings of Shakyamuni Buddha who, in his great compassion, provided something for everybody. To some people practising Pureland the fact of personal incapacity — bombu nature — is pretty obvious whereas to others it takes some arriving at. The latter often practice some other form of Buddhism first. Many of the great Pureland masters in history did so. They came to Pureland in the end after years of trying to enlighten themselves by strenuous meditation or rigorous vinaya discipline or profound textual study in some other branch of Buddhism. A relatively modern example of somebody who did the same thing within the Pureland tradition is Kiyozawa Manshi who drove himself to the limit trying to find out if it was really true that he could not do it himself.

We should remember the example of Shakyamuni Buddha. He had his self power period, which was his period of asceticism. It was at the point when he despaired and took the rice milk offered by Sujata that faith awakened, dependent origination was understood and flowers fell from the sky.

> Striving to know why his mother died
> he cut off the milk of human kindness
> and punished himself til the ribs stood out;
> then, receiving a sincere gift,
> he let love in
> and changed the world.

Buddhas Exist

Question: "Buddhism is the belief that beings do get enlightened. Arhants and Buddhas do exist." How can we truly know that? I don't know that I've ever met an Arhant or a Buddha. Am I even capable of knowing if I have?

Short answer: Seeing is believing.

Longer answer: The Buddhist movement began with and was spread by people who had met a Buddha called Shakyamuni. The whole tradition is a transmission of that particular charism. The truths taught by Buddhas are universal and are still true whether a Buddha appears to teach them or not, but the establishment of an actual tradition depends upon a Buddha appearing. Therefore, one evidence that a Buddha has appeared is the existence of this remarkable tradition that has transmitted the Dharma through 85 generations to the modern age.

> *"I met some real saints, and that is good enough for me."*

When Dogen went to China he came back inspired because he had met a teacher who he thereafter referred to as "the old Buddha". My own teacher, Kennett Roshi would say that when she went to Japan she saw some good practice and some awful practice, but along the way, "I met some real saints, and that is good enough for me."

People are attracted to Buddhism primarily because they see there people who have something that inspires them, liberates them and encourages them. I know people who, because of their Western education, are highly sceptical of much Buddhist doctrine, who, yet, attend Buddhist events because they have met Buddhists who have something that they want — a happiness, inner strength and tranquillity.

Faith, in Buddhism, does not stand opposed to experience. It stands upon a foundation of experience. Seeing is believing. The Buddha set out to create a cadre of people who would be a light. Their influence would bring peace, compassion and wisdom to the world. Of course, not every person who espouses Buddhism immediately lives up to this ideal. Nonetheless, I have met many great teachers and great souls. I did not agree with everything every one of them said, but I felt the quality of inspiration — the charism of Buddha — that flowed in their veins. It is that living faith that matters, not assent to intellectual propositions.

If I had not met Chögyam Trungpa, Kennett Roshi, Ato Rimpoche, Thich Nhat Hanh, Minh Chao, Saiko Sensei and others, then I would only know of Buddhism as an interesting theory in books. Buddhism is a living transmission. However, all of these great figures living the Noble Way in the midst of samsara are enlightened beings inasmuch as they are living the Dharmakaya. Their existence leads us to the unavoidable intuition of the Buddha as a property of this and all possible universes – the Cosmic Buddha, if you like. Each nirmanakaya great soul is different, has different character and different upaya because this is the conditioned world and we live here amidst diverse circumstances, but all are part of the same work. To worship one Buddha is to worship them all.

Ritual and Message

Question: A Sangha member recently asked, "If Honen's teachings are so simple, why are our services so complicated?" As the Sangha member noticed, our services have lots of words, bells in the right places, and ritual. How does this fit with the simplicity of Honen's, "just say the nembutsu"?

Short answer: Ritual can be as simple or as complicated as you like. The simple message within it remains the same.

Longer answer: In Pureland, ritual is not a means of achieving something, but of celebrating. In that sense it is a kind of party and you can have a big party with lots of activities or you can have a little party with not many elements. This is the fundamental point. Tangentially, nonetheless, ritual does achieve various things. It acts as a focus for the community, bringing people together in ways that promote harmony and enables us, in a variety of ways, to express our faith together. Hopefully there will be elements in the ritual that reach a variety of people — singing, praying, reading, bowing, offerings.

Secondly, it acts as a training ground for character development as people learn to co-operate, follow, take the lead, and even compensate for each other's errors as the performance unfolds. Thirdly, while the ritual revolves around a single, simple message, it also speaks a range of sub-texts that act as auxiliary practice, supporting our primary faith. Thus nei quan and chi quan deepen our appreciation of the meaning of "Namo" and of "Amida Bu" respectively.

> *"People went to stupas... to receive blessing and grace."*

Making offerings reminds us of the beginnings of Buddhism when the Buddha would arrive in a village or town as a guest and people would receive him and hear his teaching. The offerings we make are the things one would give to an honoured visitor. Doing walking nembutsu reminds us both of the spiritual path journey and also of the earliest tradition of circumambulating the stupa. People went to stupas to pay respect to the Buddha's relics. This was both to remember and honour the great sage and also, by presence and association, to receive his blessing and grace into one's life. Each element of ritual has some deep meaning or history encoded in this way. Participating becomes a way of enriching our lives. When we do not understand the code it may seem unnecessarily complicated, but when we do understand the meaning it becomes a wonderful way of immersing oneself in the richness of the tradition and associating with all the great figures who have, down the ages, spoken these time-honoured words.

We should also note that it is up to us individually or collectively how we perform our rituals. They are not an imposition. Each temple and each community will do it a little differently, but they all draw on a common stock of ancient meanings, most of which are common to the whole Buddhist world and not merely to one school.

The So-Called Marks or Signs of Being

Question: I am new to Pure Land Buddhism and would be grateful for information on the place within this tradition of The Three (or Four) Marks of Buddhism:

> Impermanence (anitya)
> Suffering (dukkha)
> No-self (anatma)
> Liberation (nirvāṇa)

Short answer: I'm not aware of a distinctively Pureland treatment in the tradition, but I can offer one.

Longer answer: The fourth of these — "Liberation (nirvana)" seems to have been added later. If we concentrate, then, on the first three, I think it is a mistake to take this original set — anitya, anatma and dukkha — as equivalents, as in the type of translation that says "everything is impermanent, everything is suffering, everything is not self". The original text says

> sarva samskara anitya
> sarva samskara dukkha
> sarva dharma anatma

Now it must be apparent that there is an intended contrast between the first two sentences and the third one. All samskaras are impermanent and are dukkha, but dharmas are anatma. This is not, therefore, a list of things to be taken as all descriptive of the same thing. In fact, samskaras are readily identified in the Buddha's teaching as a source of trouble and Dharma as a source of salvation. So, I submit, the virtually universal normal interpretation is wrong.

What are samskaras? D.T.Suzuki translates the word as "confection", most other commentators as "mental formation" or something similar. Confection is closest etymologically. They are the things we cook up in our head, the stories we tell ourselves, the complexes of our mind. What is Dharma? Dharma is the truth, what is fundamentally so. I suggest that this text tells us that the stories we tell ourselves, all redolent with selfreference, are ephemeral and cause trouble and that the truth has nothing to do with self. Liberation and nirvana are the result of deeply realising this and having faith in it.

Is there anything especially Pureland about this interpretation? Pureland is, in many ways, a very practical application of the non-self teaching. 'All Dharma is non-self' makes sense. Different Buddhist schools try to bring us to it by different routes, Pureland simply by having us accept that salvation is not self-generated, but is an other power. The Sanskrit passage above — a statement of Buddhist central doctrine — is wholly other power in its main import. It clearly says that Dharma is not self. Of course, "not self" means other.

So, the samskaras are the ordinary mentality that is focussed upon things that are impermanent and troublesome whereas the Dharma is focussed upon what is not impermanent, not troublesome and, most importantly, not self. This is what constitutes liberation and nirvana.

Guilt

Question: What is the right attitude to have toward feelings of guilt?

Short answer: It is unproductive and wasteful of life to attack oneself for being what one is.

Longer answer: First we must distinguish between guilt feelings and objective guilt. Secondly, we must take into account that guilt and justification have a particular role in our culture due to our history of monotheism on the one hand and ancient Greek and Hebrew ideas about justice as the highest good on the other. Thirdly, guilt feelings are closely bound up with pride and conceit in that much of what presents as feelings of guilt is really an assault by ourselves upon ourselves for having generated evidence that we are actually not the type of person that we want to believe that we are. Our self ideal says one thing and the evidence says something else and we prefer to punish ourselves for betraying the truth so that we can continue to hang onto our illusion. Another way of saying this is that we do not want to face our shadow.

Human nature is deep and complex and derives from a long evolutionary and karmic history. We have within us all shades of tendency. We are angels and devils. We cherish, preserve and protect life and we are destructive and murderous.

We respect one another, the other's rights and property and we are rivalrous, avaricious, greedy and prone to take what we have no right to. We speak words of love, kindness and compassion and we gossip, lie, weave skeins of half-truths, tell exaggerated stories and stir up quarrels. We are sexual beings who express love and care with our bodies in delightful ways and we lust after all manner of satisfactions that we know would bring pain and trouble to others. We enjoy healthy habits of life but are also extremely vulnerable to compulsions and addictions of many kinds. In the course of our evolution humans have destroyed many other species, fought innumerable wars, raped, pillaged, desecrated, betrayed, abandoned and destroyed and, correspondingly, have also been the victims of all such iniquities. All this is in us. Taken as a whole we call it the shadow.

> *"We do not want to see the impulses within us that lead us toward becoming victims and persecutors."*

Generally speaking we do not want to look at this side of ourselves. We do not want to see the harm we do and especially we do not want to see the impulses within us that lead us toward becoming victims and persecutors. We do not want to see our own greed, hate or arrogance. However, the paradox is that the less willing we are to see the shadow side of ourselves the more likely we are to act it out in subtle ways without realising what we are doing. We then find ourselves in a position of feeling guilty or of deceiving ourselves about the evidence before us. However, such feelings of guilt are themselves just another way of making victims of ourselves and such deception only feeds the repression that leads to further acting out. Typically, therefore, ordinary people who have done little or no insight work are caught in cycles of self-waste, squandering their life energy in the effort to expunge the evidence of the reality of their nature.

The problem is particularly difficult in a culture in which the prevailing metaphysic has been one that believes that at the end of life one will be held to account for everything that one has done with terrible consequences awaiting whosoever is incapable of justifying themselves before the ultimate tribunal. The problem is easier in Buddhism because there is no such Judgement Day reckoning. Karma accumulates piecemeal and each wilful act brings its own consequences. Thus Buddhism sees error where judgement religions see sin. It is relatively easier and less damaging to accept that everybody makes errors than to see everybody as a sinner. In the early form of monotheism, although we are all sinners we could rely upon God's mercy, but as belief in God has weakened we have tended to abandon the salvific aspect without losing the judgemental part which is rather unfortunate. Even those who no longer believe are all too often still burdened with the condemnatory half of the attitudes that correspond to the supposedly abandoned creed.

> *"As we realise our own vulnerability and susceptibility to error so we can better appreciate that it must be the same for everyone else."*

The solution is, therefore, to look deeply into our nature and see both the yin and the yang of it. This enables us to see that all are in the same boat and as we realise our own vulnerability and susceptibility to error so we can better appreciate that it must be the same for everyone else. From this flows fellow-feeling and mutual understanding, something that our world is much in need of. It is by this means, rather than by the inculcation of guilt, that our world will become a more loving and peaceful community.

> I'm not so clever
> my judgement is poor
> and I judge myself harsher than all.
> It's true I did do that terrible thing
> and many another beside
> so now...
> I am your brother forever.

Faith and the Eightfold Path

Question: If everyone is equal in the assuredness of their place in a Pure Land, does this not discourage people from efforts to behave nobly (e.g. following the Noble Eightfold Path)? How does this relate to the Buddha's teaching of the Four Noble Truths?

Short answer: The Eightfold Path is a natural outcome of true faith and nobody enters the Pure Land without faith.

Longer answer: In the West we are used to the kind of religion in which the reason for doing good is to reap a reward in heaven. However, in Pureland, we are told that heaven is specifically for people who are not perfect. It is not presented as a carrot to induce good behaviour.

The only reason to do good things is that they have good outcomes. That is why they are called "good". While we only do good in order to please a divine figure, we remain children, unable to make our own judgement. The Buddhas do not want to keep us in an infantile condition. They want to help us to grow up. When we do so we find that, on the one hand, the Buddhas are close at hand, yet, on the other, we really are alone. We make our own judgements. What the compassion of the Buddhas gives is a vast spaciousness. Reflecting that heaven, we give space to others naturally.

> "What the compassion of the Buddhas gives is a vast spaciousness."

In my understanding, the Eightfold Path is a description of the life of an enlightened person. In other power spirituality we have faith in the saving grace of such people. The more faith we have, the more our life comes naturally under their influence and inspiration and, naturally, the closer one's life then approximates to the Eightfold Path.

The idea that the Eightfold Path is a way to arrive at enlightenment, however, is a mistake. The Buddha did not become Buddha by following the Eightfold Path. He discovered the Eightfold Path by becoming enlightened. The Eightfold Path is an outcome, not a means. We do not have the ability to follow the Eightfold Path by our self-direction. The actions of deluded beings are deluded.

The correct understanding of the Four Truths is as follows. They are correctly called Four Truths for Noble Ones.

1. Dukkha is a truth for noble ones. This means that noble ones are not free from dukkha. Noble ones are noble precisely because they accept and face dukkha rather than running away from it.

2. Dukkha-Samudaya is a truth for noble ones. This means that for noble ones things (emotions, thoughts, impulses, etc.) come up. For ordinary beings this leads them into distractive, escapist, ego-centred or self-destructive behaviours. For the non-spiritual person, therefore, dukkha-samudaya is the origin of more dukkha. However, noble ones are capable of unhooking themselves and handling the emotions differently.

3. Dukkha-Sumudaya-Nirodha is a truth for noble ones. This means that noble ones are able to handle the emotions that come up. They are able to do so because they have faith and so do not panic. They trust that all is well.

4. Marga is a truth for noble ones. Marga is the eightfold path. This means that the outcome of the above three steps is that noble ones are on the path.

The correct understanding of entering the Pure Land is as follows. Every Buddha has a "Buddha field" or "Pure Land". This is the field of influence of that Buddha's great merit, just like the magnetic field around a magnet. When we enter such a field we get magnetised too. We become little magnets. In order to enter such a field we have to turn our hearts toward a Buddha. The Buddha who is said to be most accepting is Amida. This is because of the nature of the vows that he made. Therefore, Pureland Buddhists turn to Amida and have faith in his saving power and thereby enter into his field. All who do so will eventually, naturally, walk upon the Eightfold Path. There is nothing discouraging about entering the Buddha field of Amida Tathagata.

It is a mistake to assume that the purpose of religion is to make people conform to a specific standard of behaviour. This kind of idea puts the cart before the horse. The Buddha says that good behaviour might well be what an outside observer first notices about a spiritual practitioner, but what is behind that behaviour is an attitude of mind, an orientation of feeling, a deeper faith and wisdom.

Behaviour is an outcome and a symptom of deeper changes. Strictly speaking, it is incidental to spiritual awakening.

> With the body
> comes much trouble,
> nothing unnatural in that.
> Yet with the trouble
> comes an opening
> to the Land of Bliss

What is Nembutsu?

Question: In Pureland we say the nembutsu all the time. Can you say more about what nembutsu means?

Short answer: I, a foolish being, cry out to Amitabha Buddha.

Longer answer: The word nembutsu is Japanese and is made up of Nem and Butsu. Nem (written nen in the compound) means "mindfulness". Butsu means "Buddha". So nembutsu is mindfulness of Buddha. However, it has come to mean not merely a mental act but also a verbal one. Thus all formulae of refuge in Buddhism are forms of nembutsu. Furthermore, nembutsu has come to mean especially mindfulness of the Buddha Amitabha, the Buddha of all acceptance, and this implies a very wide and generic approach to spirituality.

Consequently, the uttering of nembutsu is an exceedingly widespread practice in East Asia. When I was in Vietnam, people could see by my clothes that I was some sort of religious practitioner and one could see by their gestures that they were asking what I was. When I said "Namo Adida Phat" which is the Vietnamese form of nembutsu, all was immediately understood with smiles all round. They knew I was Buddhist. Similarly, if I meet Tibetan Buddhists and they ask what is my practice and I say "Om Ami Dewa Hrih", or say that I am a devotee of Amitabha, they know exactly what I mean and we are friends straight away. In the West we tend to be much more concerned about sectarian differences because of our unfortunate history. It is nice to let all that go and just enjoy the variety of ways there are of practising. The form of words ("Namu Amida Butsu" in Japan, "Namo Omito Fo" in China, and so on) vary from place to place, but the spirit is the same. In English, we generally say Namo Amida Bu, but there are many variants.

> "Bit by bit, unconsciously to ourselves, a transformation occurs."

Buddhism tells us that that mind is conditioned by its objects and the best object is Buddha so saying the nembutsu in one form or another is very healthy. It is also a community unifier. In our Sanghas we say Namo Amida Bu as a way of saying "Hello", "Goodbye", "Thank you", "Gosh", "Never mind" and so on. It means that in all the little triumphs and disasters of daily life the Buddha is present. Thus, just as fine rain eventually saturates an overcoat, our fearful minds are gradually permeated with a beneficent influence and bit by bit, unconsciously to ourselves, a transformation occurs. When life ends we shall be naturally inclined toward going home to the Buddha Land.

> To you who have travelled so far
> to hear the secret wisdom
> all I have to offer is,
> Namo Amida Bu.
> Let it do its secret work.
> Do not travel in vain.

The Power of Mantras

Question: We had an interesting discussion about the sacred syllable OM used in so many religions (Hinduism, Jainism, Buddhism...) Someone said that in a mantra, OM could be replaced by any other sound since we are the ones who give a sacred power to the word which in itself means nothing. Some seem however to admit that the syllable has in itself a certain vibration which is beyond what we may attribute to the word. Also someone said that the only function of the recitation of a mantra is to pacify the mind and its endless discourse, so the words in themselves are of no importance. I would very much appreciate your comment on the matter.

Short answer: There are many dimensions to this, not just one right one.

Longer answer: I don't think that any of these positions encompasses the whole matter — there is some justice in each, but none is enough on its own. Words are not entirely arbitrary. Take the English word "fish". It is certainly suggestive of the movement of the animal through the water. It seems probable that music preceded speech in the sense that our most remote ancestors probably sang to each other a bit as birds do. Suggestive sounds would be at a premium in such communication. The part of the brain that deals with musical sound is in the right side of the brain. In the symmetrical part of the left brain we store vocabulary. Gradually words and verbal vocabulary evolved and became more and more elaborate and nowadays much is relatively arbitrary, but that is a modern (i.e. in the last ten thousand years or so) development.

The specific sound OM, or perhaps it might be better written Aum, is said to encapsulate all the sounds that humans make. If you say it slowly you will notice that your mouth starts off wide open and gradually closes as you go through the range of sound. This, therefore, is not a purely arbitrary syllable. "Gosh" or "Ouch" would not do the same job— though they do do other jobs quite well. Since Aum encapsulates all sounds it is the mother of speech. This is what gives it its special, divine quality.

"A mantra is a protection for the mind."

Of course, it is the disease of our age to overrate our control, power and rationality. Nonetheless, intention does make a difference. In a phrase like Namo Amida Bu, the actual words are less crucial. It is the intention that they express that matters. In a different country you find different words doing the same job. No problem. So long as one intends what one says to be an invocation of Amitabha Buddha, any suitable words will do.

As for the function of a mantra, it is a protection for the mind. This functions in a number of ways. In the case of a mantra like OM there probably is a resonance with something deep within our archetypal psychology. Then, any mantra builds up and becomes a key to a host of good associations. The single syllable thus becomes a trigger linking one to a great spiritual wealth. The fact that the same words have been used from time immemorial also adds weight to this effect. One is connecting with the ancestors and their power. At the most simplistic level, while the mind is full of the mantra it is not full of other less wholesome things.

So I don't think that the answer to your question is just one simple point. There are many dimensions to what is at work. The mantra does its work upon us and we remain mostly unconscious of the effect. It keys into us at a deeper level than the merely rational. I imagine that it reaches something on the right side of the brain.

> Om
> is the centre of the universe, they say
> while to others, "A rose by any other name..."
> Yet sweet it is
> to say holy words
> and praise the Holy Name.

Amidist Nembutsu

Question: What is specific to the Amidist approach to the nembutsu that might distinguish it from the approach of other similar schools?

Short answer: Nothing.

Longer answer: Nembutsu is refuge. Taking refuge is the core mystical act that defines Buddhism. It is the only practice that all Buddhist schools have in common. To take refuge in one Buddha is to take refuge in all Buddhas. However, different Buddhas show different facets of Buddha Nature. Amida shows primarily the facet of all acceptance. Therefore Amida Buddha is a favourite Buddha for ordinary people. Pureland Buddhism derives from the Buddha's teachings directed to ordinary folk. We understand Pureland, therefore, to be an original form of Buddhism deriving from the earliest times. We, therefore, take refuge in Amida Buddha and we commonly do so using the formula "Namo Amida Bu." We do not see this as essentially different from any other form of taking refuge such as may be practised in any school of Buddhism.

However, while there is no difference in essence, there are differences in style and focus. The emphasis, when one takes refuge in Amida, is upon acknowledgement that the being who seeks refuge needs to do so because of being a "foolish being of wayward passion", a vulnerable, limited, deluded, error-prone mortal. Here, therefore, there is a recognition that we each manifest greed, hate, pride, worry, sloth, and a wide variety of forms of self-centredness and that, although we might improve in some areas, the fundamental propensity to give rise to such characteristics is indelible and we are, therefore, incapable of achieving our own salvation by our own self-directed efforts. This recognition adds extra power and urgency to the impulse to take refuge. Taking refuge comes to have the sense of turning to a salvific power that we ourselves lack.

"Nembutsu is refuge and refuge is Buddhism."

In this act of taking refuge, therefore, there is a profound sense of letting go and of relief. We see the self-perfection project to lie in ruin, but we also feel a great gratitude for the presence and support of the Buddha who sees us in our actual state and loves us just so, even as we are. This is deeply moving. In the West we are used to thinking that religion is about moral strictness and secular society is about doing what we want, but in the East this attitude is reversed. There, it is recognised that it is actually secular society that disciplines us whereas when we go to the temple, Amida accepts us just as we are. A main characteristic of a Buddha is unconditional acceptance so it could not be that Buddha is a harsh judge.

Our Amidist form of nembutsu, therefore, is a devotional and emotional practice, something that touches the heart and that links together all those who are similarly moved. This linking generates a sense of community and fellowship. Amidist practice, therefore, is often more communal, singing together rather than sitting in isolated silence. There is a place for solitude and silent contemplation, but I am pointing out here a difference of emphasis in style. Reciting the nembutsu together we not only take refuge in the Buddha, but find refuge in the Sangha in a palpable sense too.

Fundamentally, therefore, nembutsu is refuge and refuge is Buddhism, and Amida Buddhism merely asserts this basic faith. In style our practice is less perfectionist, more devotional, more communal, and more emotional and it has its own distinctive ways of understanding core Buddhist teachings in accord with this orientation.

> Say the Name in ecstasy
> Say the Name in fun
> Say the Name in deep despair
> Say it to the sun
> Say it to the moon and stars
> to every one by one
> Say the Name by day and night
> in dire, mundane or happy plight
> til heaven comes in sight.

Benefits of Nembutsu Practice

Question: I wanted to know how I could deal with the bad karma and delusions which cause me great pain in this life, whether or not there are practices or ways of chanting to receive benefits within this life.

Short answer: Nembutsu brings measureless benefit here and hereafter.

Longer answer: There are two ways in which we suffer from karma. One is that the conditions of one's life may be adverse. The other is that one is attached to old wounds, defeats, blows to pride, rejections and so forth, cruelties that are not actually operational in the present, but which one finds it hard to relinquish. The practice of nembutsu chanting brings relief in respect of both kinds.

In the case of adverse circumstances, turning one's mind to Amida brings one into a larger scheme of things. Present difficulties are seen as transient and relatively less huge — just blips in the cosmic scheme. The more deeply one takes refuge the less important one's poverty or oppression of circumstance appears. The more clearly one sees the bombu nature of oneself and others the more one experiences a fellow feeling for all of humanity. As in all schools of Buddhism, benefits derive from giving merit away and caring for others — love, compassion, sympathetic joy and equanimity.

In the case of attachment to the past, the practice of nembutsu enables us to know that it is precisely to beings in the kind of state that we are in that grace comes. There is no particular need for us to shed our past. In fact, we have far more past humiliations than we think. Karma is fathomless and we have been battered in infinite ways. In the aeons of time the tears we have shed would fill oceans.

Thus nembutsu brings all kinds of benefit. It makes us part of a loving and compassionate community both here and beyond. When we turn to Amida we receive the Tathagata's infinite blessing. This is what Buddha has vowed, so we can rely upon it completely. In regard to the present we feel relief. In regard to the flow of time we feel confidence. In regard to the past, we make it our offering to the Buddhas — they know better than we what to do with it. In regard to the future we feel assured. All is completely assured. Namo Amida Bu.

How Do We Proceed?

Question: Dear Dharmavidya, I've just read your writing on contrition. As usual, you always know how to get right into my heart! Contrition is indeed born from honesty. Admitting our bombu reality is so freeing. However, I'm caught in the self power/other power quandary. If we accept our bombu state, how do we proceed? Do we still strive while knowing we can never do it "perfectly"? To some the bombu paradigm doesn't gel with our bootstrapping indoctrination. How have you navigated our perennial tightrope walk?

Short answer: When we really accept our bombu state we know what to do.

Longer answer: As a bombu, I do not ask "What can I do for the universe?" even less, "What is the universe going to do for me?" but rather, "What is reality asking of me today?" This is no different to Zen Master Dogen saying that the enlightened life is dictated by the miscellaneous circumstances of daily life. Real acceptance of non-self power means (1) giving up self-aggrandising ideas about what one is going to become or the spiritual achievements that one is going to accomplish, (2) knowing that the Buddhas will give one all the realisations and awakenings that one actually needs if one will just get out of the way and give them half a chance, and (3) in the meantime acting on whatever faith or insight one already has.

> *"Accepting one's bombu nature is a big climb down, a big relief."*

This last step seems simple, but actually takes great courage. Accepting one's bombu nature is a big climb down, a big relief, and also a letting go of excuses. In fact, life is mostly one mistake after another. The attempt to be always in the right or to get a perfect formula is self-defeating. There is too much going on. The attempt to always be in the perfectly balanced attitude is paralysing. When we walk along it works because we are always off balance. If we were not we would not move forward. The art of Buddhism is not to stand stock still, but rather to use the imbalance of life to flow onward. Thus the Buddhas take us just as we are, not in a state of frozen fear of getting things wrong.

"Just as you are" means that the Buddhas are already with you. Whether what I have to do today is counsel a dying person, wash the laundry, travel to Peru, or dig the garden, this is all holy work. All Namo Amida Bu. It is holy work and therefore I am unworthy to do it, yet I must in order to be sincere (true to what I know so far) and I can because the Buddhas are with me and they lend me their power. In the process I gain no merit worth talking about, I make nothing of myself, but the work of Buddha goes on. "The life of Buddha is increasing. Do not kill Buddha." (Keizan Zanji). We kill Buddha when we aggrandise ourselves so that our little light, being so close to our face, prevents us from seeing the much greater light beyond.

When we ask for a formula about how to proceed in a general sense, are we not asking to be programmed, like a machine? And is a machine not a dead thing? Being alive, we actually proceed day by day, step by step. Each of the "miscellaneous circumstances" comes along and we respond. We respond as best we can. Responding as bombu beings we do not use the circumstance as a device for hiding. We are just what we are.

> "Celebrate the Dharma that is already in our midst."

Sometimes our response is such that we feel contrition afterwards. Sometimes joy. All manner of things. Yet each of these happenings is Namo Amida Bu, and Namo Amida Bu is both "please" and "thank you": please show me the way, thank you for holding my hand. When one has this kind of faith, then one is not looking for "a means to achieve" — we meet in our religious gathering to celebrate the Dharma that is already in our midst, the vows that have already been made, the Buddhas who already love us and all sentient beings, just as they are. I am so happy. Namo Amida Bu.

Mondo

Question: What is mondo?

Short answer: Mondo is a ritual of formal question and answer between teacher and disciple.

Longer answer: Mondo is a word from old Japanese. 'Mon' means 'gate'. 'Do' means 'way' or 'path'. 'Do' in old Japanese is the same as Tao in Chinese. Mon refers to the doubt or question in the mind of the disciple. Do refers to the path that opens up from that doubt. The master is the gatekeeper. This is the "gateless gate". Although it is a gateless gate and, in principle, the person could walk straight through without the help of a gatekeeper, in practice we help one another. The gatekeeper has already been through the gate a few times and so may be able to assist with a perspective on the matter. Because of this experience, however, it may also be the case that the gatekeeper learns most, hearing all the traveller's tales of those who pass through the gate.

On the one hand, the doubt or question is a symptom of delusion. On the other hand, there is no passing through without encounter with the doubt. This is why there is the saying "great doubt, great enlightenment". This is like the grit and the pearl: no grit, no pearl.

In practical terms, mondo is a procedure that we use in retreats and courses. It is an encounter between the student and the teacher in which the student has the possibility of putting his or her personal special question and getting a response.

Preparation for mondo is also valuable. Refining the question is important. Sometimes in a therapy group we ask, "If you were going to work today, what would you work upon?" Everybody in the group considers what is his or her primary or cutting edge issue right now. Perhaps only one or two people actually do any therapeutic work that day, but the sheer act of focusing upon the question, "what is my question?" is useful.

In a certain way, mondo is the enactment of the Dharma and it does not ultimately matter whether one is the disciple or the master, each is playing their part in the opening and closing of the gateless gate, which is no different from the windbell blowing in the wind and emitting the voice of Buddha. Whether the wind blows from the West or the East, the North or the South makes no difference.

Often when we read the great texts Buddha is asked a question and in many cases the first response he gives is lavish praise for the asking of the question: "Oh well done, Ananda! Because you have asked this question it will be for the benefit of innumerable sentient beings for many ages to come." There is no one who asks and none who answers, but yet the show must go on. Hence Buddhas appear in the world and the clay mountain turns to gold.

Evil Beings in the Pureland

Question: I watched a TV programme recently that featured a rape. It really affected me and one thing that struck me was, "How would it be for someone who has faith in Pureland to contemplate that the perpetrator of violence against them could also enter the Pure Land?" It is hard to imagine feeling delight or any sense of security being in the same place or realm as one's attacker, but do we experience things differently after death or when in Pure Land? Do we even have a body to be concerned about protecting when in Pure Land? If you have any thoughts in response that might illuminate this issue, do please share them.

Short answer: Faith heals.

Longer answer: Religion heals. Christianity says to forgive, Buddha says to let go. In the Dhammapada he says:

> "He abused me, he defeated me, he cheated me, he robbed me... in those who harbour such thoughts hatred never ceases. He abused me, he defeated me, he cheated me, he robbed me... in those who do not harbour such thoughts hatred ceases. Hatred does not cease with hating, with love alone it ceases."

Now hatred is very closely associated with fear. What we fear we want to exclude, avoid or destroy and this is aversion and one aspect of dukkha. It is a very central part of Buddhism that we learn how such feelings can be transformed into the enlightened path.

Of course, we are not necessarily very good at doing this. However much I may want to be an ideal Buddhist, I may still feel fear welling up, my blood temperature rising and my muscles going tense when the person or thing that I fear approaches or cannot be avoided. At such a time I find that our Pureland faith helps me a lot. It helps me to realise that I am not in control. Even though I want something different to be happening in me, I cannot make it happen. On the one hand, this leads me to realise that I am exactly the kind of creature that Amida saves. On the other hand, it enables me to realise that the person or thing that I fear is also not fully self-controlled. This may well enable me to arrive at a better understanding of the other which may change how I feel somewhat.

"We shall heal and this will be true for others too."

Now, it is prudent to avoid being in proximity to danger. The tiger is not evil for wanting to eat me, but I am still well advised to steer clear of him when he is hungry. A Pure Land is a realm where the intention of Buddha prevails. I can be confident, therefore, that even though there be evil minded people there, harm will not come to me and that healing will take place. We all enter the Pure Land with hearts and minds that are corrupt in varying degrees and we trust that in proximity to the Buddha and bodhisattvas there we shall heal and this will be true for others too. Insofar as we can find compassion and fellow-feeling for others, this process will go quicker.

Those who enter the Pure Land full of greed, hate and delusion are not immediately in sight of the great Bodhi Tree and the Buddha at the centre of that land. They arrive inside a closed lotus because, as yet, they cannot stand the brilliance of the Buddha's light. Inside their lotus chamber they learn love, compassion, joy and equanimity. When they have done so, even if it takes a hundred years, the lotus then opens naturally and they find themselves in a great pond of other lotuses, some open and some still closed. In due course they are able to go ashore and join the other beings enjoying that land and enter into the full presence of the Buddha.

I think we can probably see that the lotus staying closed is not a punishment but a protection. We cannot approach the light of Buddha until we are ready. We need time to heal and grow in faith and confidence before such a miracle can unfold before us; before we can participate.

Nembutsu Practice and Mindfulness in Daily Life

Question: Dear Dharmavidya, how can I do frequent nembutsu repetitions and be mindful in my daily life?

Short answer: Just do it whenever you remember.

Longer answer: 'Mindful' in Pureland means mindful of Buddha, mindful of Amitabha, mindful of nembutsu. The word nembutsu means mindful (nem) of Buddha (butsu) so anything that brings Buddha to mind is nembutsu. Of course, what we more fundamentally mean is having Buddha in one's heart. Perhaps, as several people have suggested, heartfulness is a better term. Anyway, according to Honen, it all hinges on senchaku, which means making a decisive choice or selection in favour of nembutsu as one's chosen practice, after which many things come to be seen as nembutsu.

In practical terms, in the Amida Shu community, for instance, the ordination precepts prescribe saying the nembutsu in every waking hour and at least 108 times per day. In a community of practitioners this is not too difficult since we use "Namo Amida Bu" in place of or in association with "Hello" "Goodbye" "Please" "Thank you" "Never mind" "That's great" and all ordinary daily expletives — something good happens,

"Namo Amida Bu", something bad happens, "Namo Amida Bu" and so on.

"Say a million nembutsu a year."

You can also set yourself a "target". In a sense this is just a game, but, as Honen says, if you determine to say a certain number of nembutsu, it keeps you going. In the Sangha we have sometimes agreed to each say a million nembutsu in a year.

The point, however, is to be in love with Amitabha Buddha — having faith, reflecting, thinking about, having the image, feeling a sense of Buddha close at hand in all that one does and drawing strength and comfort therefrom. When this is the case you can be sure that a kind of nembutsu is going on unconsciously all the time, just as you don't stop loving somebody just because they are out of your mind while you are concentrating on some task or other.

These two sides — the deliberate conscious practice and the heart felt intuitive centring of life upon the Tathagata — support one another. Life is like that: the really important things are deep and intuitive, but they don't grow unless we feed them.

When is the Pure Land?

Question: I am confused about the location of the Pure Land in time. In some things I read, it seems to be located in the future, after death, when one "goes to" the Pure Land to become fully enlightened (and then returns to serve all sentient beings). It is an afterlife, be it ever so temporary. This is not to deny encounters and foretastes of the ultimate Pure Land here in this life, but it is to say that in its fullness the Pure Land is decidedly future. But in other things I read, the Pure Land seems to have been "demythologized" until it is (only) a state of consciousness here and now. These readings seem to be, at best, agnostic about any form of life after death. Can someone help me sort this out?

Short answer: Given that we do not know much, taking a literalist view is the simplest option and most practical in terms of one's spiritual life.

Longer answer: Yes, you will find different interpretations in different schools of Buddhism and even within schools. The literalist take is that the Pure Land of Amitabha Buddha was established ten kalpas ago and is and will continue to be in existence for a long time yet. As Buddhists we hope for a good rebirth and the best rebirth is one in the presence of a Buddha. If we are Amida Buddhists, we hope that that will be Amitabha

Buddha. However, all Buddhas have, or are in the process of creating, Pure Lands. Some people—sravakas — are happy to get to a Pure Land and stay there. Others — bodhisattvas — go there for a time, but have made vows to return to realms that are not (or not yet) Pure Lands in order to help the salvific work of the Buddhas in those domains of delusion. Pratyekabuddhas — people who enlighten themselves unaided — do not go to the Pure Land.

There are approaches to Buddhism that take it that the Pure Land is not a domain but rather a state of mind. Imaginary, but imagination that is powerfully effective in one's life, either here in this life or/and in future lives. Of course, from a subjective perspective it might be rather difficult to tell whether a Pure Land that one experiences oneself as being in was real or imaginary and even philosophically it might be difficult to define what these terms mean when what one is talking about are bardo transitions. There are, of course, also plenty of Buddhists who will tell you that this world is just imagination, too. It is possible that the question of whether experience is inside or outside of something called imagination is a complete red herring.

> "Buddhists, therefore, are naturally involved in making this world into a better place in one way or another."

From a modern physics point of view, time seems to be being regarded as a dimension of the universe and, apparently, the best fit idea with current scientific observations is the theory that we live in a cosmos that has eleven dimensions. I don't think any of us really understand what this means and based on the record so far, best scientific opinion could still change many times before we get to a point of confidence. Anyway, death is a mystery, but if you take it that the momentum of one's life continues onward then the Buddhistic ideas do seem to me as satisfactory as any even if it is impossible sometimes to sort out how literally to take them, or even what "literally" would mean in this respect.

As we say in Summary of Faith and Practice, you do not need to know all the answers to have your life usefully shaped by the faith.

In my own life, the idea that I perhaps came from some kind of realm of light before birth fits well with childhood experience that I had. The idea that I might go back to such a realm fits well with a near death experience that I had in my twenties. I'm willing to take the stories and descriptions that one finds in the sutras in the manner in which one listens to travellers' tales — as a fair description that might not turn out to be exact in every detail.

As for Pure Land in this life, I think we are not going to make this world into anything close to the Pure Land that is described in the Pureland Sutras, but, that said, if one has confidence that one has been accepted by Amitabha then one feels oneself to already be a citizen of that Land of Bliss and that being so one can hardly avoid involving oneself in acts that tend in the direction of making wherever one is into some reflection of one's true home. Buddhists, therefore, are naturally involved in making this world into a better place in one way or another. This is a practical matter.

So, to summarise, I am not for demythologising, but am not a complete literalist either since there is much that we cannot know, but if we take it that the Pure Land is the domain of Buddha and that it has existed, does exist and will exist, that in some sense it is already one's true home and that, if possible, it would be wonderful to be reborn there in the future, then this will have a profoundly positive effect upon one's life.

> When from this short life I am released
> grant me there to be born straight away
> no other bardo state intervening;
> or if it take a thousand year
> of dancing round the Holy Name
> then let it be that I am glad
> to bow and serve as called to do.

Mother Buddha

Question: Can we think of Amida as mother?

Short answer: Yes.

Longer answer: Buddhas can appear in whatever form is necessary to save sentient beings, so can certainly appear as mother. However, one has to be careful in designing one's own Buddha because there is a substantial chance that one is just massaging one's own delusions, desires, preferences, prejudices and so on. Iconographically, Amida figures are invariably male, but commonly a very gentle, soft male. However, if what was needed was for Amida to appear as a fierce dragon, I'm sure that would also be possible. Perhaps Amida has already appeared as the iconic figures of some other religions too. The female Buddha form is generally taken to be Quan Shi Yin and she is often portrayed with baby Maitreya, the Buddha of the future age. Many of these figures have a distinct resemblance to the Virgin and Child imagery of Christianity — though generally with a more cheerful facial expression. Which came first is uncertain, but this all speaks of a universal archetype.

In Buddhism, too, we talk about "parental mind" or, actually, "grandparental mind". The teacher should have grandmother mind. Grandmother is never shocked — she's seen it all before — but she is a guide to good living who has her feet on the ground and is always good for a hug when one is down or a word of gentle advice when one is in a fix.

> Amida whispers in the ear
> of every one on Earth.
> Though blind and deaf
> we all have caught
> his words of goodness
> now and then.

Bombs, Victims and Persecutors

Question: With regard to the recent *bombings in Brussels, is it better to suffer or to inflict injustice? Is it better to be the victim or the perpetrator?

Short answer: All parties need our compassion and understanding.

Longer answer: This is a complex question. Psychologically, we know that it seems to be easier for a person to be in the villain position than the victim position. This is because they are more in control. If one has done something wrong, and one then feels contrition, that is painful at the time, but one does know that one has the choice and power to live one's life differently from now on. On the other hand, when one has been the victim, one has not had such control and there may seem to be nothing that one can do to prevent similar things happening in the future, so the anxiety that sets in may be difficult to shift. However, the evidence is that the majority of people, perhaps 80%, of those who have suffered serious trauma have returned to being completely normal after a few years, so there are natural processes by which one recovers and regains confidence.

---

*March 2016

If we turn our attention to the recent bomb attacks, other factors come in. The above comments about victims still apply. Most of those who survive will "get over it" naturally and a minority may still be suffering post-traumatic symptoms for an extended period. In addition, many who were not victims in any direct sense, will experience an enhanced level of anxiety. Brussels will see less tourists in the coming couple of years. A small number of people who have been direct or indirect victims — some relatives of people killed, for instance — may feel a personal urge toward vengeance, and the general public will also be more inclined to support retaliatory action.

However, if we consider these last remarks about the urge toward vengeance and then look at the other side of the political equation, we soon realise that there must be a great many more people in the Middle East similarly affected than there are at present in Europe and this may give us some insight into why these events have happened. Why would anybody want to attack us? Well, have you noticed what "we" have been doing in the Middle East for the past several decades? Unfortunately feuding, or tit-for-tat, is a scenario that has no natural end until all the players are dead or until the cost to all concerned has come to seem so prohibitive that exhaustion sets in. We have to hope that before long "jaw-jaw" will avert "war-war" and people who at present hate each other will find the wisdom to start talking and de-escalate the situation.

> "Compassion needs to be impartial and unconditional."

The term "terrorist" basically means somebody whose intention is to create fear as a means of manipulating a political situation. In the Middle East, at present, all sides are terrorists in this sense. However, carnage in Brussels will receive much greater coverage in our press, accompanied by much outrage, than greater carnage in Raqqah or Homs, yet the feelings of victims and relatives there will be no less.

Unfortunately, this means that none of the main antagonists regret their actions and not many people feel much compassion for those "on the other side". To bring peace in such situations requires actions based on judgements that rise above partisan positions, but at present we do not see many of these, so probably the trouble is going to get worse both "there" and "here" before it gets better. It is tempting to go into a political analysis, but I am trying to confine myself to the original question.

What does Buddhism say about this kind of situation? That it needs wise compassion and that such compassion needs to be impartial and unconditional. Buddhism is not much concerned with "justice" except insofar as it believes that karma will have its natural consequences. Since karma will take its toll, the human role should be that of understanding and tender care aimed at the creation of conditions for a better future. However, when things have already gone so far, pacification is going to require serious compromise on all sides and at present nobody is in the mood for that.

So, let us try our best to avoid being victims and to avoid being perpetrators, even though, in present circumstances, this is much easier said than done, and, where possible, let us try to inject some sanity into what is at present an increasingly dangerous, multifaceted and bloody affair.

Self-Care

Question: How do we differentiate between self-care, self-help and self power? Isn't it important to do our best to look after our health, to respect the gift of life and to prevent the burden of our care falling to others? If learning self-help techniques can help us to function better in the world for the benefit of others as well as ourselves, isn't this a helpful practice, albeit secondary to reciting the nembutsu? How is self power different and why is that discouraged?

Short answer: Other Power inspires us to good work and good work requires a good vehicle, which is our own body, speech and mind.

Longer answer: It is certainly true that it is right to avoid putting undue burden upon others and that means taking reasonable care of one's body and mind. However, in the climate of our Western culture, self-care and self-help have run to rather an extreme, far beyond what is reasonable and helpful. This is not so much a matter of self power as self-indulgence. Self power refers to trying for spiritual salvation by relying upon one's own inherent qualities, but what the advertising agencies offer us is not salvation. So the first thing to say is that everything you say in your question is perfectly true, but at the same time the way that most people nowadays will interpret this goes rather beyond the literal meaning. The second thing is that it is easy here to confuse terminology. Because we talk about other power as saving grace that does not mean that other power will mow the lawn for you, do the shopping or bleach the laundry. Relying upon other power does not absolve one from ordinary responsibilities.

Self power refers really to believing that one is one's own god. It locates the source and locus of spiritual salvation within oneself. Other Power designates the attitude to spirituality that relies upon a grace coming from outside of oneself to effect salvation. In everyday terms, such grace may take many forms — there are innumerable things to be grateful for — but especially the inspiration that we receive through being close to or associated with wise and compassionate teachers as well as to that which we receive through angelic means such as visions and dreams.

"Eat when hungry, sleep when tired."

Other power inspires us to live good and noble lives and gives us a confidence that "all is assured" which is to say that we do not have to generate the outcomes directly by our own power. We can trust that whatever good we do will, in the great scheme of the universe, yield good outcomes somewhere somehow. If we rely upon self-power we feel hesitant, wondering if we can guarantee the results we intend or desire, but if we rely upon other power we do not hesitate because it is all in hands much more powerful and competent than our own. We are just doing our bit.

Nonetheless, in order to carry out any such inspiration, we need to keep ourselves in good shape. We need to eat when hungry, sleep when tired, take medicine when ill, exercise and so on. Self-care therefore comes naturally. Of course, nowadays, people develop quite exaggerated ideas about their "needs" to the point where self-care soon becomes self-indulgence until it is actually unhealthy and certainly takes up much more time, money and energy than it warrants. That is a distortion.

"Self-help" is a term deriving originally from a book written in Victorian times by a man called Samuel Smiles. It was a rather reactionary book, suggesting that if people are poor it is because they do not make enough effort. It fits closely with the "positive thinking" movement which claims that everybody can win the same race if they just want to sincerely enough. There is a grain of truth in the idea that determination can aid accomplishment, but the claim is excessive. The result is that many people feel, unnecessarily, that they are defeated by their inability to accomplish unrealistic goals in life. The fact is that, in social and material terms, people are not born with equal chances.

Sensible measures toward self-improvement are, well, sensible! There is nothing in the idea of other power to suggest that one should not stop smoking or that there is anything wrong with learning a new skill or adopting a healthy habit. Just as a parent is happy to see the child develop, but still loves the child even if he is slow, so the Buddhas are always happy to see us grow but accept us completely as we are. What this understanding does is to dissolve our sense of guilt and failure.

Self power generally involves a kind of perfectionism. It is better to be an industrious imperfectionist, than a hesitant perfectionist. No matter how much self-help we undertake, there will always be some things that we simply have to accept. From a self power point of view, that is failure. From an other power point of view it is realism and a basis for gratitude that even we, such as we are, are so blessed.

Trikaya

Question: As a Vow 22[*] student I've been asked to look at the trikaya and make some comments. I'm researching the answer but find many different answers.

Could you give me your interpretation of the trikaya and what each means to you?

Short answer: Nirmanakaya = the Buddha appearing in the world; Sambhogakaya = the Buddha appearing in spiritual form; Dharmakaya = the ultimate nature of Buddha.

Longer answer: The spiritual life is grounded upon our experience through the senses and intuition. We encounter teachers who act within the practical world; we have spiritual experiences, often as a function of such meetings; and we have an unavoidable intuition of a beyond - the ultimate, infinite, unconditional - that Buddha sometimes calls the Unborn, sometimes the Deathless. This is metaphysics, but it is very practical in that it designates our experience. Experience goes beyond the merely empirical. Our experience of the transient world inevitably generates our intuition of what is not impermanent - nirvana. However, we find ourselves stuck in

---

[*] An Amida Shu training programme

samsara. Spiritual life actually occurs in the tension between the two - the space of spirituality - the sambhogakaya. This is the realm of visions, dreams, and profound awakenings. Amida Buddha is sambhogakaya.

There is some correspondence between trikaya and the Christian trinity. God the father (Dharmakaya) is beyond our ken. God the Son (Nirmanakaya) appears in the world, teaches, relates, and engages in human life in the material world. The Holy Spirit (Sambhogakaya) thus descends upon those with faith and empowers them to go forth in apostolic mission. This is very similar to the Buddhist principle.

Those who presume to know more than can be known about the absolute are dogmatists. Those that seek to deny the absolute are sceptics. Buddhism is a middle way. Neither dogmatists nor sceptics can experience a real spiritual life. The sambhogakaya is inaccessible to them because of, on the one hand, rigidity of pre-judgement and on the other negativity of faith.

In East Asia Buddhism revolves around sambhogakaya, not just in Pureland but in the generality of the main schools. In the West there has been such an emphasis upon the historicity of Shakyamuni that many practitioners have lost touch with the spiritual level and made Buddhism into either a technical practice (which turns it into a kind of mental keep-fit) or a moral system (which puts the emphasis upon conformity rather than discovery, doctrine rather than wisdom). Buddhism has techniques and morals but they are not the core of the Dharma.

The Unborn

Question: What exactly is the teaching/doctrine of no-birth? I can only come at that through the idea that there is no-thing to be born ... only causes and conditions out of which a transient reality emerges. And that reality is ultimately all of the causes and conditions: it is where the entire universe comes into focus, and not a "thing" which is born. Is that reasonably close to the teaching of no-birth, or am I far off? Namo Amida Bu.

Short answer: Dharma has no beginning.

Longer answer: Well, all that about no things existing, only conditions, is probably well and fine, if a bit too abstruse for most folk. Everything is impermanent except something. That something is, in Buddhism, called nirvana. It was never born and it will never die. You could call it the Tao or the origin of God or whatever. It is that in which all mystics take refuge. When we hang on to impermanent things we are inevitably compromised and our soul is corrupted. But if we do not do so, in what shall we take refuge? In Udana 80, Buddha says, if there were no Unborn, no Unconditioned, no Deathless, there could be no liberation. There is no complete conceptual way of defining this. One can only hint. However, this is what all mystics of all religions turn to and rely upon.

I think that there has been a tendency to overlook the mystical truth of Buddhism and reframe it as a theory of quasi-physics or ontology or morality. Buddhism is not really about the nature of being, it is about salvation. If I put my trust in the Unborn, then my life transcends the limitations of physical being and my manner of being in the world is in accord with the Buddha Way because it is not compromised. This teaching is the teaching of a higher loyalty.

Ideas about causes and conditions and all that are not meant to make one accept that there is nothing for it but to just be a product of conditions. They are meant to show us what a perilous position we are in. Causes and conditions are the flames of the burning house. Do not waste time.

The Deathless

Question: I think I broadly understand deathless. The state of no rebirth and therefore no more death? How does deathless differ from immortal? If there is no more birth and no more death surely this is immortality?

Short answer: The Deathless is nirvana.

Longer answer: Not everything is impermanent. The Dharmakaya — absolute truth — is neither born nor dies because it is not dependent upon conditions. It is unconditional. We, on the other hand, are mortal beings living conditional existences. How can we bridge the gap? How can the unconditioned speak to us conditioned beings? All true religion is concerned with offering something toward answering this question. All the Dharma of Buddha, all the appearances of bodhisattvas and sambhogakaya Buddhas — all these are generated by this tension.

Dogen Zenji says that it is not really that a deluded person becomes an enlightened person because there is no continuity between the two. The enlightened person is in continuity with enlightenment without beginning. It is a different realm. Yet the realm of enlightenment totally interpenetrates the realm of ordinary conditioned life. They are not two different places.

The Pure Lands of Buddhas are intermediate realms. They are not the Dharmakaya itself because they are still conditioned realms. The conditions are much more favourable, but not totally transcended. Also one enters the Pure Land for a time. There are limits.

Buddhas live in the perspective of the Dharmakaya and we have faith in them. Thus we have faith in the deathless. Shakyamuni forbade us from speculating too much about such things as immortality. What we already are is enough.

Was Buddha Self Power or Other Power?

Question: As I read the sutras from the Nikayas much of what the Buddha teaches seems to be very self power — try hard to concentrate, do this, don't do that — I'm having trouble squaring this with the Pureland teachings and wondered if you think they were just a later development in the Mahayana canon or if it's due to mistranslation of the original sutras, or something else?

Short answer: It is a matter of how you interpret it.

Longer answer: The Buddha catered to a range of different people. He taught ethics and mind training, but he was always at pains to say that there is something more beyond that. This "more" is usually called prajna. People often take it that the ethical and mind training parts are the main substance, but in fact it is the prajna that takes one beyond. Prajna is seeing beyond all the relative things. Ethical behaviour is intrinsically good and it is what the outside observer sees, but it is always relative. Mind training goes deeper, but again it is relative. Buddha says that a person can master all the dhyanas and still be deluded. You can go on training your mind forever.

Prajna is different. It is complete faith. Emptiness. All acceptance. It is not relative. You have it or you don't. However, the people who came to see the Buddha were not always ready for that so he employed skilful means tailored to the case. Take the case of the young Brahmins who come and ask how to get to Brahma. Buddha teaches them to meditate spreading love, compassion, joy and equanimity. These qualities are all expressions of faith. While one is fearful or cynical one cannot do it. Take the encounter with Angulimala. Buddha essentially says, just trust that it will be OK and you can change your ways. If we have deep faith we will do the best we can in life because there will be no reason not to. Faith takes away all one's excuses and anxiety.

It is a total mistake to think that other power implies passivity and inaction. Rather it takes away hesitation and worry and inspires us to get on. It is not about avoiding making effort at all. It is freeing. If I think that my salvation depends upon my own effort and behaviour then I have to be exceedingly careful always to do the right thing and the practical outcome is that I do less. If I think that salvation is not in my hands, but that the Buddha will support me, then I am free to do things and make mistakes and learn.

"Our salvation is being taken care of by Buddha."

Of course, as you know, I do have issues with some of the translations and renderings of texts into English. To take a very topical item, I take 'mindfulness' to refer to having one's heart and mind full of Dharma. This is faith. The common contemporary way of taking it is as a skill to be practised by suitable effort and attention. In other words, it is presented as a self power practice or training, when, in fact, in my view, it is a matter of turning oneself toward other power. Buddha believed that right faith yielded good behaviour, good thoughts, good intentions and so on. He did not think that good behaviour etc. on their own would do the trick. When we put ourselves into any kind of strait jacket — even a good one — we rebel. The path to true goodness lies through having a deeper faith.

We have an unfortunate tendency to assume that religion exists to manipulate us into right behaviour against our will. When we think like this we lack faith. We are not trusting, but seeming to see a devious motive behind the teaching. If we realise our limitations but realise that our salvation is being taken care of by Buddha, then we become free. It is liberation.

So, no, I don't think that Pureland was a later development. It is the original teaching of Buddha, especially his teaching to lay people.

> He sought to conquer when he was young
> and got many a wound in the fight.
> When he was older he gave others the gain
> and won many hearts instead.
> When he fought alone, the gods looked on;
> when he turned around they came to his aid.

Dukkha-Dukkha & More Dukkha

Question: Does the common Theravada and Tibetan Mahayana teaching of three levels of suffering have any place in Pureland?

1. suffering of suffering (Pali: dukkha-dukkha) — obvious physical and mental pain and our emotional reactions to it
2. suffering of change (vipariṇāma-dukkha) — the suffering implicit in pleasant experience because of its transience and our desire to hold onto it anyway
3. suffering of conditioned existence (saṃkhāra-dukkha) — the suffering implicit in identifying with the aggregates, which are subject to impermanence, suffering, karma, etc., and not under our much-desired control

Short answer: It is not a Pureland teaching, but Amida loves you anyway.

Longer answer: I am not aware of a specifically Pureland text that includes this formulation. Of course, I have not read them all, so you never know. However, Pureland is not really predicated on an assumption that the name of the game is to eliminate suffering except in the general sense that nobody wants to suffer more than they need. However, that said, it is evidently a central point of Buddhism that there is dukkha and in different schools one finds many different ways of classifying it. So I will comment on this Theravada classification from an Amida Pureland perspective.

The first two are fairly self-explanatory — there is pain and there is the fragility of pleasant experience. Buddhist art often focusses on the second and this is the basis of the style that in Japan is called yugen. This is akin to the western idea of bitter-sweetness: the cherry blossom is doubly touching because any minute it is likely to be blown away and lost forever. This is the taste of life. Samskara-dukkha I would interpret taking samskaras to be "internal formations" or "mental confections". Buddha says that these are dukkha. From a Pureland perspective, we can say that these are what constitute the major part of our bombu nature — our foolishness.

> *"One will never eliminate dukkha. This is what Buddha discovered."*

This classification does seem to underline the fact that dukkha is not eliminable in this life. All three kinds of dukkha are going to accompany one throughout one's life, no matter how many realisations or awakenings one experiences along the way. No matter how ascetic one becomes one will never eliminate it. This is what Buddha discovered in the years before he woke up. Neither the most luxurious indulgence nor the most extreme practice could take the dukkha away. Only by faith in the Way of the Tathagatas could one hope to live a noble life and find oneself naturally upon the path.

So the basic Pureland perspective on this will be that Amida Buddha has a special care for beings like ourselves who suffer from all of these kinds of dukkha, that one is not going to cease to do so and therefore it is good to turn to Amida and rely upon his saving power.

Buddha and Derrida

Question: Derrida is famous for saying that "there is nothing without a context" and I wondered whether his thinking partly overlapped with dependent origination.

Short answer: Definitely, but... not everything is impermanent.

Longer answer: Buddha's teaching emphasises that all ordinary things — abstract as well as concrete — are dependent upon conditions and therefore subject to change, decay and death. Many people in the West take that part of his teaching as the whole of it. However, the other half of his teaching is that there is a possibility of liberation and liberation is a matter of identifying with what is not conditional and not impermanent. He called this by a variety of terms, but the most well-known is nirvana.

In this sense, we could say that most Western Buddhism is philosophy rather than religion. It is Buddhism with the "salvation" taken out. That, of course, also means that the whole of Buddha's fundamental intent is ignored. Presumably this is because we live in an ultra-materialist age.

Within the philosophical domain, Buddha and Derrida would, I suppose, have agreed on this point. All ordinary meaning derives from context more than substance. This is clear logically as well as empirically. When one asks what something means, we are really asking, in what context is it best to see it. For example, what is the "meaning" of the current troubles in France? Possible answers: 1. The proletarian struggle against the bourgeoisie; 2. A move toward the sensible management of a modern economy; 3. Reaction by a bored population who want to liven things up; 4. Over-flow of frustration that is really attributable to many other insoluble social problems; 5. The unpopularity of the government; 6. A bid for power by the trade unions, etc. It does not matter whether your choice is politically left or right, serious or trivial, historical or of the moment, in every case, one is advancing a context as "meaning", and I imagine that Buddha would agree that this is always the case.

Buddha might add, however, that this exercise can go on indefinitely. The context also has a context and so on ad infinitum. One difference between being in samsara and being in nirvana is, therefore, that samsara is a situation where the argument goes on ad infinitum whereas nirvana is "empty" because it is unconditional. In this Buddhist approach "right view" means having an infinite perspective from the beginning. This then cuts through contention. At a most practical level it often leads to the question, "Hey, people, what's the big deal? Do we really need to get so heated here?" So Buddhism brings some cool into heated situations. It takes the fever out. Buddha was a very cool guy. His context was the whole cosmos (at least): eternity.

Secondary Faculties

Question: My understanding of Pureland is that we are all bombu and therefore use the nembutsu as it's easy for us to understand. To practice more (by use of meditation or the use of other intellectual means) seems like going against this principle, is this right?

Short answer: Not quite.

Longer answer: Bombu means that one does not have the power within oneself to become enlightened by one's own means or effort. This does not mean that one is incapable of doing or understanding anything. Honen was one of the most intelligent and erudite people of his time. He knew all the books and had disciples in several different schools of Buddhism as well as his Pureland ones. It is important to distinguish between primary practice and secondary faculties.

Regarding primary practice, the point is not whether one is capable of other practices — one might be or one might not be, depending upon temperament, etc. The point is how one regards them. As a Pureland Buddhist one regards them as auxiliary practices. If they help you to practise nembutsu, then they are good to do. Error arises if one starts to think that the other practice is going to make one into an enlightened Buddha. It won't. If one starts to think so then one has joined a different school. If one believes that one will become a Buddha (one day) as a result of turning to Amida for help then one is a Pureland Buddhist.

> *"Improving life for oneself and others... is not a means to enlightenment, it is a natural expression of it."*

Regarding secondary faculties, there are innumerable things that one can do to improve life for oneself and others. Build houses, read Shakespeare, grow roses, meditate, eat a good diet, give to charity, keep fit, learn another language, etc. etc. None are essential, but each has some merit. It is generally a good thing to use whatever health of body and mind one has, including the intellect, keeping them in trim and making the best contribution one can to culture and the common good. This is not a means to enlightenment, this is a natural expression of it. The Pureland schools in Japan all run universities and encourage people to make the best they can of their lives, but not to let doing so take over as one's prime purpose.

When one does things because of one's religious faith one has a wholesome and whole life that all hangs together. When one does similar things instead of having faith, one's life becomes fragmented. When one thinks that the reason for religion is to induce people to do the "right" things, one has the cart before the horse. When one thinks that religion is a substitute for action one's cart has no horse. Faith comes first and many other things are drawn along behind.

When one relies upon one's own power fundamentally, one has no secure refuge, but when one has a secure refuge, such powers as one has should be put to good use. Personal growth is not the meaning of life, but it is nice when it happens.

All in all, faith should open one up, not close one down, yield a vast vista, not narrow one's mind. The light of Amida penetrates everywhere. Go with that light and you will have an expansive and wonder-full life.

So, if meditation helps you to practise nembutsu, do it. If it gets in the way of nembutsu, stop it. If improving your intellectual understanding helps you to get closer to Amitabha, go ahead. If it puts you further away, don't do it. In particular, if it makes you start to puff yourself up and start to think in terms of your own wisdom, be careful. In fact, the people who have been really great intellectuals generally come, thereby, to know that the amount they understand is as nothing to what remains hidden. I have spent all of my life studying. I find it an excellent practice. It humbles me. There is so much we do not know. I spend a good deal of time writing. Again, it is a kind of personal therapy. I get things out of my system and that makes more room for the good influence of the Dharma.

Amida Pureland and Other Practices

Question: I have been at an event this weekend led by a teacher of Tibetan Buddhism. The teacher taught about the four immeasurables: loving kindness, compassion sympathetic joy and equanimity. She also taught tonglen meditation and lojong mind training. I found some of the meditations very moving. Are these helpful auxiliary practises for Pureland Buddhists or should we solely concentrate on the nembutsu like Honen and Shinran?

Short answer: Yes, they can be helpful.

Longer answer: Each school of Buddhism centres its teaching on a particular perspective upon the Dharma, but these are like windows that all look into the one big Dharma room. If one's school is Pureland, then "the nembutsu is a window through which the whole universe of Buddha's teaching can be perceived in all its depth". If one were Zen, then zazen would be the window. If one were Nichiren then the Lotus Sutra would be one's window, and so on. First choose your window! Having chosen nembutsu, then other practices become auxilliary to that. Tonglen is about exchanging self and other and all the mind training of the Tibetan system is about enhancing one's capacity for compassion. In Pureland we do not see such enhanced capacity as itself being a road to enlightenment, we see it as the expression of faith applied in the world. If one has faith then one wants to be involved in Buddha's Great Work, so all manner of enhanced capacities can be useful. So, for us, this would be an auxiliary practice.

In tonglen one gives one's merit away and takes on the suffering of others. This is very similar to the Pureland idea of transference of merit. Amida takes our suffering and transfers merit to us. Our own puny stock of merit is then unnecessary, so we give that away. We transfer it. Thus "we are dedicated to the practice that all may enter the Land of Bliss".

Secretly Taking on the Sufferings of Others

Question: Can you tell something more about the verse, "Bring help and happiness to all other beings, and secretly take upon myself, all their harm and suffering." (From The Eight Verses of Geshe Langri Thangpa in the Nien Fo book of the Amida school.) People say to me: I don't want to take the harm and suffering of others on me, I can't bear this; it is not healthy to do this.

Short answer: Buddhism is not about one's personal advantage.

Longer Answer: Of course, most people do not want to take on the suffering of others: most people are not bodhisattvas. Amida Buddha would happily take on our suffering if it would relieve us of it. When one loves somebody deeply and that beloved person is suffering, one naturally feels, "I wish I could take it upon myself and relieve them of it." To some extent we do all do this - we suffer with somebody and thereby give them some relief rather than leaving them to suffer alone. We do things that cost us time, money, health, energy and so on in order to help those we love. If a friend is in desperate straits, perhaps we give them some money — now they have what they need and we are worse off so we have taken some of their suffering onto ourselves. We might even arrange for them to get the money without them knowing where it came from. When one listens to another person talking about their distress, one takes some of it upon oneself and thus eases their burden. One could, of course, have just said "I don't want to hear about your problems — it is not good for me," but we don't. In the long run it is best for everybody that one is compassionate.

> *"The bodhisattva does not defend himself at the expense of others. By taking on their suffering he brings peace into the world."*

There is a story about a Buddhist hermit who was well regarded by everybody. One day a young woman in the village became pregnant. She did not want to say who the real father was, so she told people that it was the hermit who had seduced her. People went to see the hermit and told him what the woman had said. All the hermit said was "Is that so?" The hermit's reputation was ruined. When the baby was born the parents of the girl brought the baby to the hermit and said, "This is your baby." The hermit said, "Is that so?" They left the baby with the hermit and the hermit looked after it. Eventually the girl could keep up the pretense no more and confessed the truth of the matter. The parents came to the hermit and apologised and said that he was not the father of the child. The hermit just said, "Is that so?" They took the baby away and the hermit got on with his life and practice. The story is probably apocryphal, but it illustrates an important principle. Sometimes good things befall us and sometimes bad ones. Sometimes we are understood and sometimes misunderstood. Sometimes other people dump their troubles upon us. Sometimes they take them away again. The bodhisattva does not defend himself at the expense of others.

By taking on their suffering he brings peace into the world. This may not be apparent in the short run and he may be misunderstood, but he is not in it for himself. By doing so secretly, he does not take credit for himself.

The Eight Verses are not a text from the Pureland tradition. They are an important text in Tibetan Buddhism. There is a related practice called tonglen. Traditionally this is a practice of great compassion for others. As with almost every aspect of Buddhism, in the modern world many teachers have introduced a distortion into the practice by making compassion for oneself primary, but this was not the original form. The modern world is a culture of self-care and self-concern, but traditionally the bodhisattva ideal is one in which one abandons or renounces self and lives in the service of others. This is a challenging ideal. The most thorough text on this is the Guide To The Bodhisattva's Way of Life by Shantideva. It is a prayer to be able to be whatever it is that others really need. It is the ultimate in unselfishness.

In Pureland, we acknowledge these ideals, yet at the same time also acknowledge that as ordinary beings we often lack the courage, will power, compassion or understanding to fulfil them. We might like to be bodhisattvas, but we find that all too often we are primarily concerned with ourselves. We do not want to undertake anything that might be disadvantageous to ourselves or unhealthy for ourselves. Materialist and consumerist ideas have made selfishness into a virtue to such an extent that many people nowadays are completely blind to any other option and find teachings like these a shock. To the modern person it seems self-evident not only that people do put themselves first but that they should do so. From the Buddhist perspective, however, this is a major mistake.

One of the big problems in the world at the moment, for instance, is the fact that people from rich countries do not want to help people from poor countries and do not want them to come into the rich countries because if they do the people in the rich country will have to take on some of the suffering of the poor immigrants. This is understandable, but it is not Buddhism.

Religion or Psychology

Question: Is Buddhism a religion or a psychology?

Short answer: Both and more, but religion firstly.

Longer answer: Buddhism is first and foremost a religion, and as such it has given rise to culture and civilisation, including systems of education, psychology, community building, politics, arts, literature, poetry, and so on. If Buddhism were not a religion then it is rather unlikely that it would still be in existence today, or that it would have come into existence in the first place. One would not go through what Siddhartha went through simply for the sake of an academic or professional discipline.

Similarly, Dr. Ambedkar was the leader of the untouchables in India. He saw that the caste system was (and is) deeply embedded in Indian society. He tried to get rid of it through politics and failed. In the end he decided that only a change of religion would be sufficiently fundamental to bring caste to an end so he converted to Buddhism. Religion is most fundamental. People dedicate their whole being for religion and that is what Buddhism takes. You can take it as only a psychology, or only an education, or only a culture, but you will not get the heart of it that way.

> *"Only a religion leads people to dedicate their whole lives."*

Buddhism has come to the West through a variety of channels, but it is often appreciated here for its psychological aspect. Of course, we also appreciate its arts and its influence for peace in the world and other fruits that it has borne. However, none of these would exist if it were not fundamentally a religion because only a religion leads people to dedicate their whole lives in the way that Buddhist monks, nuns and priests do. They are not just doing a job. Thinking of Buddhism as psychology may well help a Western person to understand some important aspects of it. It can be a way in, but that way goes a lot further if one is willing to follow it all the way.

Modernism has given us much, but it also has some pernicious aspects. One of these is its tendency to fragment and then asset strip. It tends to plunder rather than deeply appreciate the cultures it encounters and turn their fruits into consumer goods. People who are only casually interested may well appreciate Buddhist art or may well benefit from the latest meditation exercise without having to make any serious commitment of their life, but if nobody makes such commitment then the wonderful fruits of Buddhism will soon not be there for the picking because the root and trunk of the tree will be dead.

In my own life, Buddhism has always been firstly a religion. I became a social worker in order to practise "right livelihood" because I was Buddhist. I got involved in various forms of social action for similar reasons. That led me into psychotherapy and, naturally, I wanted to apply my Buddhist principles in my work. That led me to write books about Buddhist psychology. Foremost, however, I am Buddhist and that is what I teach and advocate and that is what has provided the inspiration for all my most important work. Namo Buddhaya. Namo Dharmaya. Namo Sanghaya.

Obedience

Question: What did the Buddha say about obedience?

Short answer: Pay heed to the Dharma.

Longer answer: The definition of a Christian monk is a person who lives a life of poverty, chastity and obedience. Poverty and chastity are important values in Buddhism too, but what about obedience? The word obey is closely related to a word for listen — to heed what you are told and carry it out. A disciple of Buddha is called a shravaka, which literally means a listener. The basic duty of a Buddhist is to pay heed to the Dharma and put it into practice. I remember talking to a person about their relationship to their teacher and this person said, "Rimpoche never told me to do anything, but from time to time, he would say, 'Would you like to do so and so?'' If you said 'OK, I'll do it,' you found yourself more and more deeply involved. If not, not." I think this exemplifies the matter quite well. As a teacher I make suggestions sometimes. I do not mind whether people take them up or not, but if they do then they get more deeply involved and if they don't, well, things take longer. In Buddhism it is not a matter of surrender. You keep responsibility for your life and your sense of responsibility deepens. The teacher gradually gives you more. The teacher may be doing something and the good disciple notices and helps. The person who is wrapped up in himself does not notice and is too preoccupied to be able to do much in any case. That person needs more time. Thus, in real Buddhism there is no punishment except for collecting the natural consequences of one's own actions. In a Buddhist community the teacher is like the Queen Bee. The Queen Bee does not give instructions, but all the other bees are dedicated to supporting her work and making it easier. In one sense, the Master is just another human being living in the community, but in another very important sense, the community is simply those people who want to help, learn from, support and be with that teacher.

Live with Wholeness of Heart

Question: How do I proceed to live your Amidist take on the Four Noble Truths and Eightfold Path?

Short answer: Live wholeheartedly.

Longer answer: In my understanding, the Eightfold Path is an outcome. You can try to mimic it if you like, but one is bound to do so with one's deluded mind unless one is enlightened and if one were enlightened it would come naturally anyway. Really it is a description of how a Buddha lives, which is to say, wholeheartedly. This gives a clue. If one lives wholeheartedly, even the mistakes one makes will be instructive — in fact, they will be more instructive than one's successes, generally speaking. So one answer to your question is "one mistake after another", while yet keeping faith through it all no matter what comes along.

The four truths are not so much a practice as a description that liberates. They tell us:

1. that dukkha is a truth for noble ones. This means both that (a) the path is not a matter of eliminating dukkha but of learning through it and (b) that the 'noble one' accepts, faces and learns from the afflictions that inevitably arrive in life, rather than running away from or hiding them.

2. that when there is dukkha there is samudaya which is arising energy and this energy can go different ways. It can go into escapism and compulsive avoidance, into actions such as retaliation that are destructive, or into constructive, equitable response. For instance, as we get older physical dukkha tends to get more and more prevalent. That can ruin one's life or it can, at the other extreme, generate saintliness, wisdom and great compassion.

3. that the noble one is able to use the arising samudaya energy constructively because of having diminished or let go of 'self'. This is a matter of faith and of 'accepting one's lot' in a deep way. Everybody has faith – it is just a question of 'in what?' When it is faith in 'self' it is only a little light that does not let us see very far ahead. When it is faith in Buddha it is a great light. If one has faith in one's body, for instance, well, it fades. If one has faith in eternity, it lasts a long time.

4. that when we walk in the great light we are naturally upon the Eightfold Path whether we know so or not.

> *"Light comes from the Buddhas, not from our base instincts."*

So, whether we are hale or sick, young or old, dukkha happens and if it did not happen there would be no spiritual path. The path arises out of our feelings of compassion and love that spring up when we encounter the suffering of others. All of us have such impulses. We also have other impulses too. The latter include rejection, gloating, cruelty, greed and so forth. Again, do not think that you are going to eliminate them. With good socialisation one learns to keep them in check, but there is always a shadow side to the mind driven by envy, fear, jealousy and pride that delights in the misfortunes of others. The energy of anger and of resolute noble action are the same energies. Simply the application is different. What makes us go one way rather than the other? Faith that overcomes fear.

Thus another way to look at the four truths is to say that most ordinary people are trapped in the cycle of the first two. Dukkha and samudaya are truths for everybody. The energy that comes up when we suffer dukkha then becomes the source of more dukkha. The things we do to get revenge or bury our head in the sand, blame others or distract ourselves — the common worldly ways of coping — tend only to make more dukkha. The noble one, therefore, is, in Buddhism, somebody who meets dukkha without multiplying it, without making trouble for himself or others, without re-sowing the pernicious seed. That is the essential meaning of the third truth. Nirodha implies putting a bank around the fire so that it not spread. In this basic principle of having the fire stop here and not spread one has the gist of the Buddha's way. Buddhism is saying that by doing this one intensifies one's life as well as becoming a light for the world. That light comes from the Buddhas, not from our base instincts.

To do this takes faith. One has to have confidence that "All shall be well," and to have that one has to have a much larger perspective than the immediate ups and downs of life.

Duality & Nonduality

Question: In one of your recent posts, you made the statement, "Nonduality is a dualistic theory." I was hoping you could elaborate a bit more on this statement, or perhaps point to a sutra or previous work where this is discussed. It is definitely a point which would be considered provocative in some Dharmic circles.

Short answer: Nonduality is a negation and negation automatically creates a duality between itself and what it negates.

Longer answer: There is certainly a good deal of talk about "nonduality" in Buddhist circles and it is often advanced as though it somehow defines what Buddhism is all about. However, it is difficult to find any quote from Buddha himself to this effect. Of course, a lot depends on what one means. The term nonduality simply means not-two-ness. One is, therefore, obliged to specify which two things one believes are not really two — earth and heaven, subject and object, me and you, relative truth and absolute truth? Nonduality always points at a duality and asserts that in some sense it is a unity. The basic form of a duality is "this" and "not-this", hence, "duality" and "non-duality".

So generally nonduality is taken to imply "oneness". However, the term itself is constructed as a dualistic term. To be non-anything implies that there is a something else that it is not. Nonduality stands in a dualistic pairing with duality. If we define Buddhism as nonduality (I don't, but for the sake of argument...) then we are defining it as different from duality. In other words, we are asserting a dualistic scheme of things in which nonduality is one part and duality is the other part. Generally speaking in these theories, duality is the empirical part and nonduality is the metaphysical part.

In an Indian context, nonduality is a Hindu idea. In the Indian languages it is advaita (a-dvai-ta = not-two-ness). According to Wikipedia, Advaita "is an ontological approach to nondualism, and asserts non-difference between Atman (soul) and Brahman (the Absolute)." Buddha, however, rejected all of these ideas. The Wikipedia item is worth having a look at as it shows what a huge range of completely different ideas fly under the "nonduality" ensign, "Are all of these different nondualities nondual?" one is tempted to ask.

Nonsingularity is probably an easier theory to defend both empirically and philosophically than nonduality. Nonsingularity would assert that there is nothing that is truly singular, nothing that cannot be divided into parts. Buddha in particular was an analyst. He divided things. Buddhism is full of lists of parts — five skandhas, two truths, three signs of being, seven enlightenment factors, six paramitas, and so on. It was not Buddha's style to assert oneness.

Furthermore, analysis can be very practical and helpful, whereas oneness tells one almost nothing. This and that are one... so what? How does that help? It might give a cosy feeling, but it does not aid practice. It might be thought, for instance, that if we believe that "all people are one" this will make for peace in the world, but it is not at all clear how this will really lead to any concrete action, whereas acknowledging that there are many different kinds of people in the world can readily lead to thought about how to accommodate those differences and meet different requirements.

Another similar fallacy is the equation of "relatedness" with "identity". I have many times heard it said that things are "one" because they are "inter-related". However, to be related items have to be separate. It takes two or more to relate. In any case, the idea of inter-relatedness is overdone. Many things are related in a purely one way fashion. The fact that A depends upon B does not imply that B needs A in any way, necessarily.

I do not believe that Buddha taught that everything is "one", nor even that all things are inter-related, nor inter-dependent. All such ideas tend to undermine ethics because they imply that the bad is just as necessary as the good. Buddha was more for keeping things distinct and making choices with right intention.

Those who assert the theory of nonduality do so in order to distinguish themselves from others who they think have got things wrong. That, however, is a dualistic thing to do. We will get much further by being openly dualistic — or, better, pluralistic — and respecting one another in all our differences.

> *"A "polytheistic" approach has many more possibilities"*

Sometimes people have profound spiritual experiences and speak of them in what one could call "nondualistic language". They might say, "I felt connected to everything." I have no objection to this as it is simply a mode of self-expression. When the person has digested their experience it will stand out for them as something special, something not to be forgotten, something different from ordinary life. They will thus be plunged back into the duality of ordinary life versus peak experience. Their "nondual" experience will have set up an even greater duality for them. There is nothing wrong with this. Such contrasts are the foundation of religion and wisdom.

Does it matter? In principle, whether your metaphysical stance is one of duality or nonduality might not seem to matter much, but in practice there does seem to be a tendency for monisms to become intolerant. We can see this with many monotheistic sects. Even within Pureland Buddhism this danger exists. There are some people for whom Amitabha has become virtually a monotheistic deity and such people are often rather narrow whereas there are others who see Amitabha as one Buddha among many — a favourite one, but still one amongst many — and this seems to me a much more open, and tolerant position. It is also the correct position, since in the Amida Kyo which is recited regularly in all schools of Pureland there are a huge number of Buddhas listed. Such a "polytheistic" approach has many more possibilities for integrating differences and building community amidst diversity. Again, the sutra says that those in the Pureland spend their time making offering to other Buddhas in other realms. The whole idea of respecting other Buddhas is vitally important. It provides a scriptural basis for inter-faith harmony.

So, all in all, I rather think that it might be better to drop all this talk about nonduality and face up to the plurality of worlds, Buddhas, people and tasks to be done.

To Err is Human, and We Do Not Stop Being So

Question: After a good few years of working hard towards personal improvement and continually tripping over myself, I'm struggling to see any real change in my propensity for being foolish. Given the depth of my defectiveness, how realistic is it to expect a significant change at the human level?

Short answer: Wrong target.

Longer answer: To err is human. It does not end. Insight might grow, but that is not an end in itself. Insight might give rise to boredom, however, which could be useful. There is an inevitable self-contradiction — and, therefore, self-defeat — in the notion of "self-improvement". However, while we are "struggling to see", the Buddhas can see us perfectly well already. We do not need to do their job for them, just play our own part.

Actually, viewing from the outside, an observer might well see great improvement in you at the same time as you yourself find more and more reason to despair. It is not self-improvement that is required, only a diminution in self-concern. From that might well flow various observable virtues, but it is not by directly cultivating them that Dharma arrives. They are symptoms and by-products.

This is why teachers say, "Just do the practice and there will be no need to worry." Chasing after an improved view of oneself is futile. Sometimes, when we examine ourselves, we see virtues and sometimes vices, but it is all just a hall of mirrors. In the morning I do my work. At lunchtime I prune the roses. In the afternoon I do a different job. In the evening I eat my dinner. Namo Amida Bu. Namo Amida Bu. Have I "improved" in the process? Who knows! It is not my concern.

Mixing Practices — Cultivating Friendship

Question: Most weeks I visit a local temple in my town, where Theravada monks have a brief service before spending about 45 minutes meditating. This then makes me feel that maybe I should have made the effort to travel to the temple of my own form of Buddhism in a more distant town for the service there. It is quite difficult for me to travel so far at the moment due to work and other commitments. I suppose the problem I have is clinging to one practice rather than allowing myself to absorb all of the Buddha's teachings. However, as the Buddha that I am devoted to is never mentioned in the Theravada services I feel as though I'm not staying true to my faith. The alternative is that I don't go to any service and don't meet with other Buddhists. Meeting with others with the same or similar beliefs helps me. I learn and feel a warmth that only my faith gives. I'm trying to be a good person and to learn about my faith and I am learning the way that others celebrate. I hope that this is a right action.

Short answer: Mix and match.

Longer answer: All Buddha's teachings are good and there is value in having flexibility in one's practice. There is nothing wrong with singing hymns in a Christian church. At the same time, there is a great value in associating with those who have a similar form of practice and faith to oneself. The solution, therefore, is to do both. Sometimes go to the convenient temple and sometimes make the effort to go to the one that has the best fit. One can learn everywhere and, as a Buddhist, one can practise devotion to the Buddha in any Buddhist temple. The presentation of the Dharma may vary from place to place. Some presentations may go deeper than others and none is perfect. As a lay person, the best course is to learn everything you can from every opportunity that presents, but also align oneself with a Sangha that, as best one can judge, most truly represents the path in a manner that works for you. I have often been in this position myself. There are not so many Buddhist temples and the nearest may not always be the one you need most, but that does not mean that one cannot make excellent friends there and participate in the good spirit, even while, whenever possible, going elsewhere in order to cement one's main Sangha connections.

Here in France we have the reverse situation. Each week I hold a Pureland service and give a teaching at Oasis, a Buddhist community nearby where most people follow Tibetan Buddhism. There is also a Zen master who gives teachings at the same centre. This ecumenical spirit is excellent. When they can, the core group of people go to see Tibetan teachers who live further away. Last weekend they went all the way to Strasbourg to hear the Dalai Lama. This is all fine. Buddhism should give an example of friendship to the world and this means friendship between Sanghas as well as between individuals.

Many Right States of Mind

Question: How can I attain the right state of mind?

Short answer: There is no right state. The mind is a river.

Longer answer: Body is not reliable, mind is not reliable. Let body and mind "fall away". So long as we are obsessively worrying about our body and mind we are slaves to chance circumstance. The body and mind mostly work fine when left to their own devices.

If we have corrupted our mind it will not be cured by further deluded tinkering. The right state of mind is whatever is appropriate to what is going on at the time. Awe is a fine state. To stand under the stars at night and look up at the vastness of the cosmos or to look at natural beauty is food for the mind nature. One can try to include such things in the mind's diet. Attention to the task in hand is a fine state. This is something that one can cultivate, but best is when it comes naturally because one is doing what one believes in. Sleep is a fine state. There are many fine states of mind, but they are finest when they arise naturally and, mostly, the important thing to do with the mind is to stop doing things to it and let it get on.

The mind is like a great river. Its currents find the best path to the ocean. We can produce a greater calm by throwing a dam across it, but sooner or later it will overbrim our dam and go on its way again. It knows its way already.

The Merit in Being a Hermit

Question: Is there any value in being a hermit?

Short answer: Yes, huge.

Longer answer: The hermit does not have the distraction of the deluded world. In nearly all the great religions there are hermits. In the theistic religions, being a hermit is the best way to give total attention to God. Buddha's advice was, keep good company, but if you can't find any, then dwell "lonely as rhinoceros". By good company, he did not mean sociable drinking companions, he meant people who were truly holy and inspiring.

Being a hermit is a bit like fasting. When one fasts, after a few days you start to think, "Why ever do we waste so much time on the whole food thing?" You experience a kind of cleanness and clarity. The same is true with being alone. Being alone is having a people fast. Modern people in Western countries almost never experience what it is for the stomach to actually be empty, so the inside of the body is never clean and never stops working. Having a people fast is similar. The inside of the mind becomes empty and gets to have a rest. Natural functioning is restored.

Alone one will learn many things that it is virtually impossible to learn when ceaselessly in company. The whole

Buddhist path is framed within a knowledge that one could always leave society and go into the forest or the hills and be alone. Nowadays this is more difficult. There are simply too many people on the planet. When one can find the possibility, however, take it.

"To be liberated is to be alone."

When alone one can see all one's games and compulsions more clearly, both to do something about them and to get perspective upon one's foolish nature; one can feel the space and enter into a kind of free fall of faith and communion with nature and the divine; Buddha was enlightened when he was alone.

One learns how much of one's energy has been wasted on the manipulation game — trying to hook others and avoid getting hooked oneself, or searching for somebody who can hook one into a mutually desired phantasy. To break this habit is a real liberation.

Being in the company of good Sangha and being alone are more similar than either is to being in the company of worldly people. As a Sangha we have deep respect for one another which enables us to have the ekagata (singleness) that Buddha teaches as the core of practice. In worldly society people are continually manipulating and pressuring one another in order to salve their own social anxieties and cling onto their image of how things should be.

To be liberated is to be alone. It is to be alone even when in company. It is not to be needy. When one can really be free in such a way a vastness opens up. Hermits who live in such vastness bring salvation to the world. They are a door to heaven, unfastened, swinging in the breeze.

How Is It to Be Alone?

Question: Dear Dharmavidya, as you used to travel a lot, to go where you're asked, to be in groups, to give workshops and talks...What is it like to have to stay in the same place, in a little community or on your own, as you do now? How is it for you to 'miss' all these activities? Eleusis, where you live, is isolated. I think that I would be scared of this isolation, although I know that we're never isolated, but the feeling can be there!

Short answer: Intensely peaceful.

Longer answer: Being alone here is rather wonderful. I welcome guests when they appear but at present I am alone with the cat and the house and the land and the sky and the deities and Buddhas, the sun when she appears and the equally fickle moon and with my own head and heart, body and breath. And with silence. At this time of year there are not even many birds, just the odd owl call at night.

You mention the possibility of being afraid... My rational mind tells me that there is a small danger in being alone. One could have an injury or a medical emergency and there would be nobody here to pick me up and whisk me off to hospital. However, I do not feel this risk. I suppose that the truth is that one is always in some kind of danger — we are mortal beings — and so one creates a threshold. When threat comes above the threshold one becomes anxious, but the rest of the time one is at peace. And the reality here is that being alone I am less disturbed and more at peace than I would be were there people around.

From time to time I get an urge to get in the car and drive to some faraway place or book an airplane, but then I smile at myself and put it aside. I know that there is a fair chance that I will recover sufficiently to travel again so it is a matter of wait and see. If it is so then I have a pleasure to look forward to, seeing my friends in faraway places once again. On the other hand, if it turns out that my condition worsens then I can remain here and enjoy this place.

It has been a wonderful thing to be here a complete year. Many times in the past I have said to myself that it would be a good thing to do, so now it is no longer on my to-do-list. It is hard to find words sufficient to say how much I love this piece of ground — the Artemis Wood, beautiful Aphrodite Field, and all the other sacred areas. The planet is over-populated and I have 16 hectare completely to myself — sometimes I am amazed at my good fortune.

The matter of "missing" is interesting. I have sometimes felt grief in my life — terribly when my parents died, sometimes acutely when relationships broke up — but although I am alone physically here I still feel that my heart is thickly populated with good friends, yourself amongst them. Actual physical proximity is good, but only one dimension of being connected. I am sure we shall have plenty to talk about when we meet again, and this will be, in part, precisely because we have been apart.

I have been looking back over my life and the years in the Amida community have had some ups and downs, but, for all the occasional drama, it feels like a supremely good thing to have done and to be part of into the future. I imagine that some people may have been envious of my life, travelling to such amazing places and meeting so many interesting people, yet the same observers would not themselves have been — were not — willing to undertake the challenges and risks involved in casting one's life upon the wind in such a way.

People would ask me to do things. I would say "Yes!" and then afterwards wonder, how? I learnt a lot that way. Really that is the essence of Zen — not just sitting in rows or putting up with sore knees, not using a technique to eliminate one's stress — it is much more fundamental than that. If one is willing, then the powers will arrange. Right now they have arranged for me to reside in paradise for a short while accompanied by a rather eccentric cat. The important thing is not to waste it.

Who knows what comes next? As Pureland Buddhists we are supposed to believe that the next life will be in Sukhavati close to Amitabha Buddha. I have some confidence in that — a kind of homecoming — but I am just as willing (and quite curious) to be sent on some other mission — the powers will arrange. However, despite its recent failings, there is probably still quite a bit of use left in my present body so whether it is here or elsewhere or once again roaming I am sure there are many more interesting experiences waiting to be undergone.

The worldly life is shaped by conditions and we all have one. The rigidities in us are given by karma and we can't escape them. However, even if much of a great tree is actually dead wood, new sprigs still appear each spring, looking as though they were the first sign of life in the whole of time.

The Happiness Trap

Question: How can one achieve lasting happiness?

Short answer: Happiness comes when it is not sought. It is neither the goal nor the means, it is a side show.

Longer answer: Happiness is a frequent, but not essential, side product of a wholesomely productive life, but one does not achieve such a life by being happy, nor by making happiness itself into a goal. To chase happiness is ignoble. Similarly, an attitude of endless optimism or blithely thinking that all will be well in any ordinary mundane sense is more likely to lead to an unproductive life and a weak character. The Buddha spoke of striving and of crossing a dangerous stream.

The Buddhas help us. Shakyamuni urges us on and Amida beckons, but we are like the man in Shan Tao's image: chased by ruffians and wild beasts we must cross the river of fire and water and the bridge is narrow.

The animals and ruffians are our inner and outer torments and obstacles. The fire and water are hate and greed. The narrow bridge is the path of faith.

Because we have trust in the Three Jewels, the crossing is possible, but we should not think that it is all going to be easy. Overly blithe people do not see the true nature of the situation, do not strive and do not make enough effort. They become complacent. They stop using their intelligence to the full and gloss over the complexities of real life.

Some of the bestselling books in the twentieth century were self-help manuals that preached positive thinking. These ideas got into popular spirituality and there has been much written about envisaging the situation that one wants and, thereby, it is said, making abundance happen. However, recently, a rash of research has shown that people who envisage a positive future tend not to rouse themselves sufficiently to play their part in it happening. Without a sense of peril, life becomes lax. This is why Buddha taught impermanence and dukkha. A measure of pessimism is needed to balance rashness.

The aim of Buddhism is a fuller aliveness, but it is a mistake to identify this too closely with happiness. Happiness is about going back to sleep. Very nice for an interlude, but not sufficient as a guide to life as a whole. Many happinesses occur along the way, but they come incidentally. Enjoy them, certainly, but don't worship them — there are more important things. To make them into the goal is a mistake and to make holding to a happy mind into a means is also unproductive.

This is the root idea behind the insane medicalization of modern life where every slight departure from normality comes to be considered a disease. All of life becomes a trail from one pathology to another. This is a kind of madness bred of a desire for an unrealistic degree of emotional control — a kind of social strait jacket. We have a full range of emotions for a reason — a lot of reasons. It is unnatural to try to abolish any of them.

It is good to live a meaningful life and to achieve anything meaningful is a struggle. If you set out to create art, build a Dharma centre, relieve poverty, genuinely become a therapist, or even build houses and grow food, you are going to encounter obstacles and problems. If you have children and try to do your best for them, it will be a struggle. If you give it all up and like Kūya wander the countryside singing the nembutsu and helping people whenever you can, it is not going to be an easy life. For sure there will be times of great satisfaction, but these will not come along as a result of pursuing nice feelings. They are by-products. Furthermore, they pass. It is not a failure that one plunge into the next round of creative struggle rather than bathe in smugness.

So, do not make achieving happiness your goal. As my teacher used to say, "A dog asleep in the sun is happy" and it is nice from time to time to be like a dog asleep in the sun — allow yourself that — but don't raise it to great importance, nor make it a cause for personal guilt when one cannot be like that all the time. If we were all like that all the time it would be disastrous. It is not a worthy goal.

In Buddhism, happiness is represented by the condition of the gods. They live in heaven and everything goes as they wish, until, suddenly, one day, their good karma runs out and it all falls apart. They then abruptly become sick and ugly, die from heaven and get reborn in some miserable destiny from which they have to find their way. In Buddhism, heaven is not the goal. One does not pray to go to the Pure Land to enjoy luxury, one prays to go there to be near to the Buddha and become enlightened to a noble life.

Does compassion start with oneself?

Question: Can I ask you a question, because I got confused in a discussion about compassion Some people were saying that you can generate compassion through meditating a lot. I said you can meditate a lot and not be compassionate because I have met people like this; compassion happens when you are brought outside yourself by something else, not by working hard on the cushion — which could be another ego project. Then they said, you have to work on yourself and be compassionate to yourself, so I said, compassion really means realising that there is no self rather than loving the self. Then they said that if self is empty, so are other selves, so who are we feeling compassion for? Then I couldn't think what to say.

Short answer: The Buddhas are busy resolving the karmic jangles that come down the generations and we can help or hinder.

Longer answer: There is quite a lot in this question. Several questions, in fact.

Compassion is an English word that is generally used to translate the Sanskrit karuna. Compassion carries the implication of feeling (passion) with (com). It is closely related to sympathy. Karuna is almost the same thing, but is usually defined as a wish. It is the wish that others be relieved of their suffering. Karuna is, therefore, a mental activity which has an other as an object. Karuna is a mental activity that tends toward actions to relieve suffering. It is possible to generate karuna by meditation techniques. One can imaginatively establish an other in one's mind, discern their suffering, and then generate the strong wish that that suffering be mitigated or eliminated. One can further imagine doing something about it. This type of meditation will help to strengthen the karuna function in the mind. So on the question of cultivating compassion through meditation, if we take compassion to be karuna, then there are effective meditations for this purpose. This does not mean that all meditations will have this effect or even that meditation is the best way to generate compassion. Fellow feeling comes primarily from allowing oneself to be moved by the needs and suffering of others or from realising that one has the same deficiencies as they do.

> *"Meditation and action should reinforce each other, or they will neutralise one another."*

Behaviour, speech and mind are a closely tied system with constant feedback from one to another. If we generate mental karuna, but do not act upon it, then the mental faculty will decay. This is because action in the world is also a powerful way of cultivating the mind. If my meditation is cultivating karuna at the same time that my actions are cultivating non-karuna, then actions are likely to win. In any case, if there is no visible fruit in action from a meditation, it is suspect how genuine the meditation was in the first place. As for meditating "a lot", it is really quality that counts, not quantity. A moment of real change of heart is worth any number of hours fermenting on a cushion. That said, it takes some time to establish deep calm and if this can be done it provides an excellent foundation for any form of meditative cultivation. The basic message is that meditation and action should reinforce each other, or they will neutralise one another.

There tends to be a slight implication in the English word compassion that the person who has compassion is in a superior position — more spiritually advanced perhaps. If we find ourselves feeling sorry for our neighbours that they are not as aware as we are, say, then we are falling into spiritual materialism. A sense of the common pathos of life is probably worth any number of hours on a cushion.

The Matter of Self

The Sanskrit word being translated as self is atma. Atma really means the bit of God in the person and the idea that the Buddha is really trying to refute is that of predestination. The general structure of Indian religion is the idea that there is a bit of God in each of us that will inevitably find its way back eventually to the great divine source. Buddha is saying that there is nothing inevitable about it. The future will be generated from the conditions that are created. If we create bad conditions, there will be a bad future. Killing leads to more killing. Stealing leads to more stealing. Hatred leads to more hatred and so on. We are not all predestined to become enlightened, though we can do so. I read the anatma doctrine as giving us total responsibility within our existential situation.

Again, the bit of God is supposedly immortal whereas all the rest is ephemeral and contingent. Buddha is therefore not saying that we do not exist, but that what does exist is ephemeral and contingent. This effectively leads to a disaggregation of the self. My body is dependently originated. My emotions are dependently originated. And so on. The conditions for one are not identical to the conditions for the other. We are complex. So are others. As one thinks in this way, all these components start to be seen as others: hence the crucial teaching, "Thou art not that". They lose their self quality. When this genuinely happens, one becomes tranquil and objective, at the same time as experiencing a vast expansion in the arena of karuna.

The idea of "working on oneself" is a bit suspect. It is a piece of psychotherapy jargon and when properly used is fine but it can mean many things, so, again one needs to check out what they actually mean. There is an unfortunate syndrome in which a person identifies him or herself with "issues" that they then like to talk about but have no real intention of resolving, and when the phrase is coupled with being compassionate to oneself I do become rather suspicious that this is co-opting quasi-Buddhist language in a not very helpful way. Generally Buddhism calls for something a bit cleaner and more direct. Polishing one's self image is not it.

> *"The idea that loving oneself is a pre-requisite for helping others is a fallacy."*

To care for another is not to care for one thing. It is to address oneself to the different currents that flow in that being and try to find a kindly response to at least one of them. This is why listening and observing is so important. A person is not just what presents on the surface. Compassion requires penetrating wisdom. Similarly, one cares for one's body in the same way as one might care for any other body one had responsibility for. There is no "-ishness" about self any more. When people talk about loving the self, therefore, one needs to get clear what they mean. In a sense it is one of those phrases that gains energy from not quite making sense, or, at least, relying upon a shift in the meaning of words.

Love, in Buddhism, is maitri. It is parallel to karuna. Maitri is a mental act with an other as object. It is the wish that the other be happy, prosperous, successful, etc. One can cultivate this through meditation and through action in just the same way as karuna. Now, for a person who has reached the stage where the self has disaggregated and become many others, it is perfectly possible to have maitri toward the skandhas (aggregates of self) without any element of selfishness being present. This is the basis of the Zen adages of the "When tired, sleep; when hungry, eat; when the bell goes, put on your robe," type. If one attempts this process the other way around, however, starting with self-indulgence, the result will be adverse, and self-deception rather than wisdom will result. So we can say that "loving oneself", or, at least, taking good (but not excessive) care of those things that others mistake for a self, is a natural consequence of spiritual cultivation, whereas indulging one's whims is something that blinds us to the very meaning of the good life. The idea that loving oneself is a prerequisite for helping others is a fallacy. They are independent.
Rider: Also, from a Pureland perspective, we would say that the contingency of all the elements of our being ensures that we remain foolish beings, imperfect in many ways. Nonetheless,

even in our foolish, imperfect state, we can live in the light of what really is immortal, which is the goodness, beauty and truth that is in the world, to which we give provisional names like tathata (suchness). We can conceive of a person who lives entirely congruent with suchness, a tathagatha, but we cannot actually be one. It is an inspiration, not an achievable goal. We live in the light and can reflect the light, but do not become the light. We should, therefore, guard against hubris. Nonetheless, if we live in that light, the consequences of our actions will, whether we know about them or not, tend to the good and this will benefit all beings.

Now, according to Buddhism, our ephemeral and contingent being operates according to the principle of dependent origination. It is not random, but nor is it pre-determined. It is a case of freedom within parameters. If we have faith in the Buddha light (or, loosely, in goodness) then we will exercise that freedom consistently in a certain way, which is a way that benefits others. There are an infinite number of ways of doing so. If we are blind to that light, we will tend to slip into following old tracks and following selfish passions. There are only a few ways of doing this, so the selfish person effectively becomes less and less free as habit closes in around him. To live a liberated life will utilise all the affective and cognitive resources we can muster.

Attachment to the Guru

Question: In Tibetan Buddhism it is well known that devotion to the Guru is an essential part of the practice. However in the Chinese Buddhism I practice, we are instructed (as I understand it) to be devoted to the Buddha Dharma and not to the teacher. In fact our monks and nuns are moved about the world quite frequently, partly so they do not become attached to a particular place and partly so the devotees do not become too attached to them. I believe that my teacher has quite literally saved my life and given me a life of much greater joy than I ever believed possible. I have a deep debt of gratitude to him and love him deeply. Not in a sexual way, obviously, but still in a very ordinary attached, human way. I love to meditate with him and I love to hear him teach the Dharma. I miss him when he's away, even though I still have my connection to Amitabha Buddha. This connection is much stronger when the master is around and I wonder if it will become more and more attenuated if I am not in his close proximity for any length of time. So here is my big question: Does this attachment to my teacher interfere with my relationship with my Buddha, with Amitabha? If I am thinking of working for my teacher rather than getting to the Pure Land, is this not an obstacle to my practice? I can use the sadness I feel when separated from my teacher as a motivation to appeal more strongly to Amitabha

Buddha, to ask him to help me with my bombu problem, but still in my heart I long to be close to my Master. Of course we will have to separate eventually. I have read of accounts of Tibetan practitioners who deeply loved their teachers and experienced great grief at parting.

So, is love for one's Pureland teacher okay in your opinion, and how do we moderate it and use it to progress rather than get stuck in it? A couple of other monastics at the Temple have cautioned me not to get too attached to the Master.

Short answer: Yes, if it helps practice.

Longer answer: There is nothing to worry about. We are earthly beings. We love and hate. Amida loves us anyway. If one wanted to achieve nirvana by self power one would want to eliminate all human frailties and attachments might count as obstacles, but as Pureland Buddhists we do not rate our perfectibility, and if attachment to the teacher strengthens one's practice then it is all to the good. As Honen says, "If lay life gets in the way of your practice, then ordain — if monastic life gets in the way of your practice, disrobe." The same applies to "If attachment to your teacher...." Of course, this may change from time to time — we are karmic beings and you never know what karma is going to throw at you next. Also, it is naturally good if the love one has for another, be it a teacher or whoever, becomes more mature over time, but this is not something one can force along.

Just remember that Amida cherishes you come what may and that he cherishes us in our frailty, not just in spite of it. Our nature is no obstacle to him. Each teacher that one has is a unique relationship and it has roots in long karmic history. "With your hook like kindness hold me, through all bardos through all lives."

Thought, Word and Deed

Question: Here is a quotation from Cesare Pavese. "We are all capable of evil thoughts, but only very rarely of evil deeds; we can all do good deeds, but few of us can think good thoughts." Is this true? If so, what are the implications for the relationships between thought, word and deed?

Short answer: I don't think it is true, though much depends on definitions.

Longer answer: I suppose the frequency of our evil deeds is a function of what counts as an evil deed. Perhaps from the perspective of Pavese it is a fairly restricted, definite category, but from a Buddhist point of view we would have to say that most of our deeds are implicated with at least a tinge of greed, hate or delusion and often it is much more than a tinge. In that sense "evil" is normal — it is samsara. Again, from the Buddhist perspective, a truly good deed would be one that carries no karma. Loosely, we might think of good karma and bad karma and certainly some consequences of our acts are better than others, but the truly "good" — what we would call a paramita — is rare.

In the Buddhist way of understanding, thought, word and deed are all acts and what matters with acts is the intention. Now we might have broadly "good intentions", but, as Freud and his followers pointed out, and the Buddha was well aware, we all have a host of hidden motives as well. We are already caught up in karma from ages past. Of course, there is also a large category of what we might call "conventionally good deeds". These are a matter of conforming to what is thought proper within one's group. When a person steps outside of these that person risks being ostracised or castigated by his or her colleagues, companions or compatriots. Such behaviour — whether conformist or rebellious — has little to do with real good and bad, but it forms the basis of most of the judgements that people pass upon others.

"Deeds take more courage than thoughts."

Again, Pavese may, in his system, have a narrow definition of what a truly "good thought" is. Perhaps, only God has truly good thoughts in that sense. In Buddhism, even the gods do not do so — only Buddhas. However, in common speech we would be thinking more broadly, in which case I'm sure everybody has some "good thoughts" in amongst all the other ones. However, I suspect that they are acted upon less often than they occur, so good thoughts might well be more common than good deeds. Deeds take more courage than thoughts.

So, from the Buddhist perspective we can distinguish two different "paths". The first, we can call (following Thich Nhat Hanh) "watering the good seeds". This is the path of relative incremental improvement. The second we can call the path of liberation. This is the path of sudden awakening, breaking free from conditioning and cutting through our karma. This latter may come as a result of insight (very rare) or faith (relatively more common but still unusual).

So, to summarise: In general, our thoughts, words and deeds are contaminated with delusion, attachment and rejection, some more so, some less. Among these are some that are, nonetheless, conducive to the benefit of others and these generate "good karma". However, the true and ultimate path is one of complete freedom, beyond our own capacity for good and bad, in which one relies directly upon the power of the Dharma which generates no karma at all.

> Classes were on offer
> leading to liberation...
> would you sell your soul for such?
> Beyond the classroom
> good deeds invoke no retribution —
> how rare! how wonderful! how free!

Can Purity Survive an Impure Society?

Question: Is society a group of individuals joined together because of their belief in self and work in self-strengthening? Is society, as a natural consequence of that self-preoccupation, immoral and impure? If the entire society structure is immoral, where is the place of a moral and pure individual in such society? Is the adjustment to and being a part of such society immoral and impure? How is it possible to be pure and to remain a part of society? Or is it that a pure individual cannot be a part of society?

Short answer: Only impure beings like ourselves can help society.

> *"The bodhisattva must sacrifice his or her own purity in order to save beings."*

Longer answer: Probably an individual who was conscious of their purity would not be able to be part of society. They would have to maintain some distance. For some Buddhists the consciousness of personal purity is important. In the case of Pureland Buddhists, we are more conscious of our impurity — our klesha nature. A bodhisattva is also a bombu — a foolish being full of impure nature at the same time as being one who has awakened to Amida's grace. In relation to society, therefore, the follower of Amida is both inside and outside, participating and non-participating (the Buddha recognised this state of samjna-asamjna as one of the highest, short of enlightenment), world renouncing and world affirming all at the same time. We are acutely aware of our nature as fallible humans and, at the same time, of the fact that we are part of Amida's Sangha, part of the Buddha's Great Vow of universal transformation. So a bodhisattva must know his or her own imperfection in order to have the fellow-feeling that is the basis of compassion. Without such an understanding one cannot be much help to the world. In effect, the bodhisattva must sacrifice his or her own purity in order to save beings.

Society is not just a group of individuals. The group is more than the sum of its parts. There is a life lived by a group that is over and above the lives of the individuals. In Buddhism, we learn to be part of something much bigger than ourselves. The Sangha group is a transformation agent for society. By living according to Dharma principles we become like a lens that collects and focusses the Buddha's power. We do not control or direct it, but by simply living Dharma lives we become the vehicle or the transmitter. Buddhas alone are not enough to transform worlds. There has to be also a Sangha.

Also, although beings are impure and self-seeking, Amida receives them just as they are. Even though we might have all sorts of destructive habits, Amida still receives us and does not judge us. Of course, we judge ourselves and that can be painful and immobilising sometimes and it can be hard to believe that we are accepted just as we are, but it is so. The only completely moral and pure individual is a Buddha and a Buddha does not see the impurity except insofar as he sees the suffering people cause themselves. A Buddha does not adjust to such a society, but sees it through awakened eyes and those eyes know only tenderness.

So we remain part of society, conscious of our impure nature, aware of the suffering around us, inspired by Amida's all-acceptance, moved by the grace that we receive through Amida's vows to perform deeds for the benefit of all sentient beings, and, through sharing this faith, creating communities that both work as a leaven in society and exemplify an alternative.

Regarding the implied question of whether a "pure" society is possible, in practical terms the answer is no. It is an ideal. As it says in the Sandokai, "With the ideal comes the actual like a box all with its lid". As practitioners we live somewhere between the ideal and the actual, doing the best we can while recognising the reality.

How Can One Keep to Principles in a Corrupt World?

Question: My question has to do with being an Amidist in the working world. Specifically how does someone who values non-self and other survive in a working world that is based on ego, calculation, competition, profit, self-centeredness etc. I am having a difficult time too with what is often called "office politics" and am not sure how to respond to that as an Amidist?

Short answer: None of us does; however, if you take a long term view, have faith, and stand by your Sangha, remarkable things happen.

Longer answer: Let us consider a historical parallel. The Quakers were forbidden to enter government service in England in the 18th century so they went into trade. They were scrupulous people and gradually got a reputation for honesty and fair dealing in a world where these were rare characteristics. No doubt people often took advantage of them in the early days and the early history of Quakerism is full of stories of their difficulties. By persevering, however, they gradually came to be recognised for their special qualities. Many of them in fact became millionaires because people wanted to do business with people who were trustworthy and several of the leading names in UK retail industries — Clarks, Rowntree, Cadbury — are Quaker family names.

> *"It is enormously helpful in the short run to have strong faith and good friends."*

It is not easy to stick to principles of honesty and straightforwardness in a tricky world and in the short run one suffers repeated setbacks by trying to do so, but in the long run it pays dividends. Our own progress at Amida Shu has been very slow and difficult at times and we have repeatedly been told by people to compromise more, but perseverance has worked. It is better to be a quality organisation than a slick one. The way to respond to pressure and manipulation or to invitations to indulge in sharp practice is to be polite and to find other ways to be nice to people, but to not be drawn into corrupt practice. It is not usually a matter of making a stand, though occasionally that is necessary. More often it is a matter of approaching things from a different angle and taking a long term view of the situation. Of course this means that it is enormously helpful in the short run to have strong faith and good friends. Meeting with others as a Sangha can be tremendously important and I do not think that Sanghas should simply be places where people go to sit in silence together — they should be places where real human meeting occurs and ideally where practical and emotional mutual help is available. This was the case in the traditional White Lotus Societies in China where Pureland grew up. If one does not have such people close at hand then some kind of e-Sangha may provide some degree of substitute. People who engage in self-centred ways do so out of confusion about the nature of life. They are just mixed-up people trying to do what seems right to them and getting into a mess because their ideas about what makes a satisfying life are scrambled. Actually they bring much trouble to themselves in the long run and one must fear for them.

Does Equanimity Imply Incapacity to Make Judgements?

Question: An enlightened being sees beauty in everything and thus enjoys everything equally. I have some doubts about this: is it really true? If it's true then should we strive towards this kind of "equanimity"? If so, how do we make moral judgements about anything and choose between right and wrong action? Perhaps there is no easy answer to this.

Short answer: Equanimity means being able to take the rough with the smooth, not being incapable of telling one from the other.

Longer answer: It would appear from the texts, especially the Pali texts, that the Buddha Shakyamuni at least did not enjoy everything equally, if, by this, we mean get equal pleasure or have equal approval for. He clearly approved of some things and did not approve of others. Have a look, for instance, at his conversation with the monk Arittha in the Snake Simile Sutta. Buddha clearly discerns what is to be approved and what is not to be approved. The idea that enlightenment results in such a non-dualistic mind that one can no longer make any judgements is a widespread modern fallacy. Equanimity does not mean that. Equanimity means that one can, in regard to oneself, take the rough and the smooth in one's stride, and not be knocked off course thereby. This is a function of strong and clear faith (prasada, anjin). Spiritual awakening gives one a clear sense of direction and faith in being true to the Tathagata's intention. A tathagatha accepts us all just as we are and loves us all just as we are, but that does not mean that he or she does not weep over some of the deluded things we do.

Problems with Ideas of Loss, Love and Attachment

Question: I'd be interested in hearing your thoughts on love and loss from a Buddhist perspective, especially as they relate to the creation of a worldview. Everyone will experience losing someone they love through either a change of conditions in life or through death. In reaction to this fact, everyone will create their own worldview. From a Buddhist perspective you can avoid suffering through non-attachment, by not holding on to what we can't have and not struggling against what we can't avoid, but where does love fit into this? The whole non-attachment thing works great until I try to apply it to the loss of someone I love. Then it all falls apart. For example, I can be with grief when a relationship fails, and not get lost in any of the usual other strategies I might have once used to avoid pain. Then grief is just grief. But I seem stuck when it comes to the thought even of a parent losing a child.

Short answer: We will love, we will lose, we will form some kind of worldview as we try to make sense of this experience, what view we form will condition our ability to love again, and whether we can love again will determine whether our life is a noble one or not.

Longer answer: I agree with your observation that everyone will lose somebody close sooner or later and that this will shape their view of the world. That will, in turn, affect their identity and their effectiveness and will condition their ability to live a noble and meaningful life. If a person has a depth of spiritual training or experience then they can put the loss in a bigger context. They suffer and the suffering is meaningful. If they do not have that level of spiritual maturity, then they suffer and believe that the suffering renders life meaningless. The spiritually mature person has faith in a greater meaningfulness — in there being meaning beyond what one can oneself discern. One has a sense of "Even though I do not see it, these things somehow fit into a bigger meaning, one that only Buddha or the gods see".

As I see it the basic meaning of life is love and love intrinsically involves a great range of feeling, sentiment and experience, ranging from bliss to despair. It permeates the most trivial, the most momentous and every occurrence in between. We are vehicles for love, mediums in which love takes place and all the currents that flow as a result are what we experience as the peak of being alive. The actual form that that takes — love of a partner, love of country, love of an ideal, love of God, etc., etc., right down to love of ice cream — will give particularity to the meaning of an individual life. Unlike most commentators, I do not take the purpose of Buddha's teaching as being that we no longer experience pain and certainly not that we be so detached that nothing matters any more. That would be a pathology, not a nobility. I think that what the Buddhas want is that we live noble lives — which means ones that are true to our love. In being so, we rise above suffering and set-backs, but it demands courage.

When Buddha teaches detachment he is teaching us to detach from our tendency to be self-serving. The real target of Buddha's attack is conceit. If I lose somebody and fall into self-pity, that would be unbuddhistic, but that I mourn is perfectly natural and proper. To grieve is simply one side of loving.

Take the simple case of being separated from the person one loves. On the one hand, one misses them. On the other hand, one feels blessed that they exist. One suffers that s/he is not here, yet rejoices that they are somewhere. By extension, were the person to die, one feels, as I feel in regard to my mother, for instance, sad that she is gone, yet blessed that we had what we had. Equanimity is like that. Initially I wept for her loss. Now I rejoice in her memory. None of this is totally cool, calm and collected, but it is real and there is nothing ignoble in that.

"By realising the universality of her lot, she found a new view of life."

When the loss is tragic, as in the loss of a child, say, the challenge is greater. Children do die. It is part of the great scheme of things. We are inclined to ask "Why did this happen to me?" which has an element of conceit in it, but what such a loss teaches us is that this is part of the human lot. If the self-pity gets the upper hand, it will destroy us; if it does not we shall find a depth of compassion that goes beyond anything we have known before. Of course, in such a situation, a measure of self-pity is normal, and there will be a natural struggle between the different parts of the person as they go through this awful experience. The relevant Buddhist story is that of Kisagotami. Note that Buddha did not tell her to practice detachment. He led her to encounter the losses that others had also suffered. By realising the universality of her lot, she found a new view of life which eventually transformed her into a spiritual teacher herself. No doubt she mourned bitterly for her lost child, but this suffering was not in vain for it was part of her transformation into one who benefits all sentient beings.

The spiritual path is tough. It is love and love requires courage and perseverance, vigour and restraint, wholeheartedness and willingness. On this path we learn everything that we need to make us into the kind of beings that the Buddhas want us to be.

Is Oneness the Goal of Practice?

Question: Famous nembutsu practitioners may be able to experience oneness, but those who have not reached that stage practise with a consciousness of things as dyadic. Sometimes new practitioners arrive at oneness quickly, but it is difficult for those who value doubt. I think there may be a problem explaining how to get from dyadic experience to oneness. I am a yoga teacher. The Yoga Sutra says:

> 3-1 Concentration (dharana) is holding the mind within a centre of spiritual consciousness in the body, or fixing it on some divine form, either within the body, or outside it.
> 3-2 Meditation (dhyana) is an unbroken flow of thought toward the object of concentration.
> 3-3 When, in meditation, the true nature of the object shines forth, not distorted by the mind of the perceiver, that is absorption (samadhi).

Dhyana became 'Zen' in Japanese. I think that Zen is a process whereby a person and object become a oneness. Samadhi is the ultimate limit of this. We cannot live in samadhi stably but striving toward it is noble. Thus Honen's nembutsu may be Zen and Shinran's may be samadhi. Both are noble. I'd like now to refer to Gendlin. He says that meditation is deep while focussing is shallow, but since he values process a lot he seems to have some negativity toward those who relax in a deep place of meditation.

A 'felt sense' will occur as a natural response when we relate to certain objects. These felt senses have implicit meanings. Discerning them we can make a good relation with the object. Focussing is thus a way of living based on consciousness of felt sense.

I think that the best relation between a person and an object is oneness. Just as we are mostly not conscious of air, when a person has the best relation to an object he or she has no consciousness of that object and no felt sense occurs. If there is a felt sense, then the person can do focussing to allay the felt sense. This moves them toward oneness. By using the felt sense, Gendlin is helping Westerners to understand real Buddhism.

Short answer: We must distinguish different meanings of "oneness".

Longer answer: I agree that focussing is useful and fits well with Buddhist practice. I don't think that focussing is primarily concerned with eliminating felt sense, but rather with deriving meaning from it, though your suggestion that oneness is a form of unconsciousness is interesting and has some merit. There are several different uses of the term 'oneness'.

There is an unfortunate tendency for spiritually minded people to assume that oneness is the goal of their practice before they have really thought what they are saying. Because of the amount of confusion that can arise, I prefer not to use the term oneness except in a very abstract way. The Dharmakaya may be characterized by oneness, perhaps, but, as soon as one says 'oneness' it tends to have the effect of preventing any further analysis or description. The word oneness is, therefore, all too often a weapon used by those who would have us stop thinking. To do so, however, implies a dangerous absolutism and I do not advise going there. Leave oneness to the philosophers. They can talk forever about it and at the end of the day will have said very little.

Generally one's spiritual life is a relationship between one's bombu self and Amida. I would not think that striving for oneness is a particularly sensible approach. I do not want to be Amida and I do not think that Amida wants to be me. I think Amida wants me to be me and Amida loves me as me not as something that I am not.

The material that you quote from the Yoga Sutra is good and practical. Some people would take "not distorted by the mind of the perceiver" as a kind of oneness, but that is not a particularly useful analysis — what is more to the point is the fact that sometimes some things strike us with such force that they overcome our old habit of mind and break us into new ground. I do not find it useful to call this 'oneness' because the salient thing about it is that one thing — me — is changed by another thing. This is basic dependent origination as presented in the Pali sutras.

In the normal sense of samadhi, I agree that we cannot live in samadhi stably. However, there are various usages. As it is used in the Pratyutpanna Samadhi Sutra, for instance, samadhi appears to be an orientation to life rather than a transient state of absorption.

Thus, samadhi may not always be the same thing as dhyana. The dhyanas (hence "Zen") are definitely transient states. They are very fine and wonderful in themselves, but even complete mastery of the dhyanas does not equate with enlightenment — it is more something that spiritual people do than something that causes one to be spiritual.

> *"The way out of the problems that dyadic thinking brings ... is to move toward pluralism rather than monism."*

Felt sense is a matter of paying attention to skandha process. Such paying attention generates a secondary process of reflexivity. Sometimes this is useful, but not always. Sometimes it is better to just receive the object than to reflect upon the process, but if the process is stuck in some way, then paying attention to it may be freeing. Thus focussing is, as you say, a corrective procedure rather than an everyday way of life. When the river is flowing we do not need to pay attention to its flow, but when it is blocked it may be useful to do so, though, even then, attention to a powerful wholesome object may be more effective than attention to one's own process. If one wishes to call that "oneness", then that is a useful form of oneness, but I tend not to think of it that way.

There is still subject and object even when one is in ecstasy. Some of this is, therefore, just a matter of different ways of using words. Much of what the Zen people might call oneness I would just call being in the flow, but I understand that flow dyadically — as a dance. I feel that this latter way of conceptualizing it is more useful. Those who advance the idea of oneness bring intelligent thought to an end, but I do not favour that approach and, as far as I can see, nor did Shakyamuni.

So basically there is nothing wrong with dyads. The way out of the philosophical problems that dyadic thinking brings, which are usually forms of polarisation (e.g. the Cartesian body-mind dualism, or the gnostic heaven-earth dualism) is to move toward pluralism rather than monism (e.g. body and mind are both complex fields; there are many heavens and many samsaric realms beyond human understanding). In the experiential domain, when we talk of oneness, if we must (and I would rather we did not) then we need to distinguish whether we are talking subjectively or objectively. Subjective oneness may be more usefully called 'flow experience' because objectively it is better thought of as a dyadic (or multi-dimensional) dance than as an indivisible wholeness.

I suggest that thinking in the way I suggest preserves both flow and doubt and makes faith a dynamic process. It enables a rich spiritual life accessible even to ordinary people whereas the setting up of oneness as an ideal tends toward absolutism, elitism, the stifling of intelligence and a loss of dynamism. It would be something limited, as you say, to "famous nembutsu practitioners" — not the people that Honen was teaching. Whether it is true or not, it is inevitably pretentious since we are bombu, not Amida. Perhaps it all appears as oneness from where Amida is looking, but that is his business.

So, if the idea of oneness helps you to make sense of things, fair enough, but 'making sense' is itself inevitably a matter of relating things and is therefore multidimensional. I myself, therefore, prefer a more pluralistic way of thinking within which the dyadic experience has a natural place. There is no need to move from this toward oneness. Of course, if all really is a oneness then there can be no such 'moving' anyway.

Is Meditation Necessary?

Question: Your, 'The Feeling Buddha' was the first book I ever read on Buddhism. It served as a great introduction to the subject and some three or four years on, I still maintain a very large interest in it as a way of life; a path. I write to you now in the hope of a response to quite a serious question that I have in relation to meditation. The question basically is: do you need to meditate to be a Buddhist? Basically I ask the question in relation to the practise of insight meditation. Over the last few years I feel I have discovered something of a way of life, a noble path which I feel I would like to try to aspire to. It's just in the area of mediation I find a problem. Many years ago I suffered from an acute anxiety episode; I was very young at the time and did feel like I was going mad — as many anxiety sufferers do. This, coupled with the experiences I have had meditating, brings this email back to my opening question: do you need to meditate to follow the path? I guess one does; it is after all the bedrock of the Buddhist faith. I just would like to know if meditation can be unhealthy in terms of mental health because if there are any such risks attached to it, I think I would rather pass on it!

Short answer: Meditation is not essential, but refuge is.

Longer answer: The simple answers to your questions are: is meditation necessary? No; and, does meditation have any mental health risks attached to it? Yes, but for most people they are not great. The Buddha clearly taught many forms of meditation but, even in the Pali literature, he repeatedly says that the various samadhis do not provide enlightenment, but only peaceful abidings or particular powers. The message seems clear that there are things to be gained from meditation, and the Buddha taught it, but it is not essential. Particular meditations provide antidotes to particular spiritual diseases, but here diagnosis is indicated, so while some self-administered spiritual disciplines may prove useful, a teacher plays an important part.

What are the risks? Well, I would not recommend meditation to anyone with major psychiatric illness as what people in that condition generally require is not more introspection, but more reality contact. I would be wary of offering meditations that involve attention concentrated upon bodily processes, such as the breath, the heartbeat, or other body functions, to people prone to anxiety states or currently experiencing major grief since this may well make them worse rather than better. For the great majority of people, however, meditation is valuable and the worst that can happen through the use of it in the vast majority of cases would be transient physical aches and pains. Having said that, I had better add that I myself had a major health emergency with pulmonary embolisms which the doctor thought — and it says so on my discharge letter — was very likely caused by too much sitting in the lotus position, something that causes the blood to pool and brings a risk of deep vein thrombosis from which embolisms are a secondary derivative. So, yes, there can be hazards, both psychological and physical.

Meditation is certainly not the bedrock of Buddhism. Buddha taught different meditations to different people and did not teach meditation to everybody. What he did teach to everybody was refuge. It is refuge that creates the condition for enlightenment, not meditation. People do not get enlightened by meditating. They get enlightened by sincerely taking refuge and 'making offerings to Buddhas'. All schools of Buddhism practise refuge. Not all practise meditation. If a person becomes enlightened while meditating it is not a result of the meditation, it is a result of taking refuge. All schools of Buddhism have formal ways of expressing taking refuge. In the Pureland tradition, one recites "Namo Amida Bu" which means that one takes refuge in the Tathagata that is in every time and every place. Other schools have other formulas. What matters, however, is whether one can really take refuge with all one's heart, not just whether one can say the words - though saying the words is more powerful than one might think. What stops us from taking refuge truly is attachment to self.

Because of this, there are all sorts of Buddhist practices that serve to loosen one's attachment to self. Correctly prescribed meditations can play a part in this. However, none of these remedies leads directly to enlightenment. They simply clear some obstacles out of the way. In principle, even a person with innumerable obstacles can instantly take refuge and fall into enlightenment and even a person who has eliminated thousands of obstacles may still fail to truly take refuge. This is because the person with many obstacles may be more motivated and the person who has supposedly "made progress" may, for that very reason, be afflicted with spiritual pride.

Do Amida Buddhists Meditate?

Question: Do Amida Buddhists meditate?

Short answer: Amida Buddhists practise nembutsu. Nembutsu is amplified by spiritual exercises.

Longer answer: Yes and no. Firstly it depends what one means by meditation. Secondly it depends whether one is asking about the core practice of Amidism or about what Amidists might or might not do in general. The core practice of Pureland Buddhism is nembutsu. Nembutsu has a narrow and a broad significance. The narrow significance is to recite the name of Amida Buddha. The broad significance is to live the whole of one's life in the attitude of knowing that one is loved, accepted and graced by Amida Buddha. Strictly speaking, neither of these is meditation as commonly understood, especially as understood in Western Buddhism, where meditation has come to signify a species of awareness exercise intended to generate insight, or calm, or generate particular mind states or virtuous qualities. However, many spiritual exercises that can be classified as meditation can (but need not necessarily) be practised as part of such a life. Thus, most of us regularly practice nei quan and chih quan, we study the Contemplation Sutra which includes instructions for a graduated visualisation of the Pure Land, and the nembutsu samadhi is an important part of our tradition. Also there is nothing about being an Amida practitioner that prevents an individual taking up a particular meditation practice as a means of combatting a particular mental problem such as stress if it is useful to them. So there are three levels to this issue. In its core, Amidist practice (or Buddhism generally, come to that) does not require meditation, it requires refuge. Those who take refuge may find a variety of auxiliary practices useful and some of these could be classified as meditations. They may also take up some practices in the same spirit that one might go to the gym or do Tai Chi and some of those might also be classed as meditation.

Having said all that, it is probably worth pointing out a few other things.

1. In the Pali texts the Buddha talks of those enlightened with and without samadhi. It is clear that samadhi is an adjunct to spiritual realisation and not a royal road to it.
2. The texts give a good deal of attention to the dhyanas but it is questionable whether what is commonly called meditation in the West fits these descriptions. The dhyanas appear to be raptures not awareness of immediate surroundings. Rapture is definitely something very characteristic of Pureland practice. I suggest that we give more attention to rapture.
3. There can similarly be considerable room of interpretation around the word samadhi. Do contemporary Western meditation methods generate samadhi? Only in the simple sense of

concentration, I think. Real samadhi is not so much a temporary state of mind as a changed vision of life. Pureland certainly generates the latter — a sama-dhi: "consummate vision" — and this change of orientation is highly consequential.

What Can One Do When Spirituality Seems Unreal?

Question: I'm going through a period where the spiritual seems not very real to me. Notions of nirvana or enlightenment seem too abstract to strive for. It is a kind of atheism I suppose, but I have always opposed that reductionist materialist viewpoint... Can you point a way forward psychologically? I still feel an affinity for the bodhisattva way, because really, life seems worthless without compassion. Help welcome. There is a way. All my intuition says so. Any opinions welcome.

Short answer: We are bound to find it so some of the time — that's the kind of beings we are. To think otherwise would be perfectionism.

Longer answer: Don't worry whether it is "real" or not and don't strive to achieve it. Simply enjoy your intuition that the bodhisattva way must be somehow right. Start with what you have got and rejoice in it.

We are here in a universe whose intrinsic meaning is too vast for us to grasp. We create lesser meanings — nothing wrong with that. Seeing our foolish nature, we conceive wisdom. Seeing our blindness, we conceive enlightenment. Each spiritual system thus generates concepts and categories to help us navigate this life and make it wholesome and even holy. In

Pureland we have the ideas of Amida, the unimpeded light of wisdom, the Pure Land, and so on. These ideas come out of fundamental human needs, but, more than that, they reflect distantly the hidden vastness. We should adopt a middle way in relation to them, neither overly literal nor merely metaphorical. They are rooted in real spiritual experience.

In Pureland, we do not strive for enlightenment in the traditional sense. We try simply to acknowledge our nature as foolish ordinary beings without thereby falling out of relationship with the intuition of Buddha that always confronts us. This seems a more modest approach, but it is actually extremely profound.

There will be times when spirit seems the most real thing there is and times when we are spiritually arid or over detached or even cynical. These states come and go. They are part of our dependent nature. Experiences in the present or past continue to live with us and we are not free of them, but we can have a faith that carries us through - a faith that even when we are not feeling faith, faith will nonetheless return. Have faith in faith. Sometimes spiritual things seem abstract simply because that is the way that we have approached them — abstractly, rather than through our own experience. We have maybe tried to force things that should be allowed to develop naturally.

As for the bodhisattva ideal it is an important part of our Amidist path. For us, Amida's 22nd vow is no less important than the other vows. Vow 22 is the one that establishes the bodhisattva path within the Larger Pureland Sutra. However, there is a pitfall here in that as soon as we start to assume that it is our task to make it so we tend to lose touch with other power, the source of grace is hidden and aridity can swiftly follow. The true practitioner is simply riding a different wave.

Delusion

Question: From the three poisons, I understand the concepts of greed and hate very well, but find delusion or ignorance more difficult to make sense of. Could you say something about it?

Short answer: Delusion is pride.

Longer answer: Delusion is the distortion of perception and thinking brought about by the "conceit of self" — attachment to the ideas we have of ourselves and particularly the tendency to regard oneself as a special case. It could be in a "positive" or "negative" fashion. By this I mean that we might have ideas of grandiosity or of self-pity. Self-power is basically a form of grandiosity. Playing the victim is self-pity. Delusion can also be multiplied up by the capacity that humans have for deception, including self-deception. Hence false humility. What presents as "guilt" may, for instance, have at its root an inflated sense of self. The person does not really regret the harm they did, they just hate the experience of perceiving evidence that they are not what they would like to think that they are.

Greed and hate can be thought of as existing at two levels. There is a basic attraction-repulsion level that is largely instinctive — as in that one likes some tastes and dislikes others. But then there is the more complex case where the attraction-repulsion is itself grounded in delusion. At this level we love what supports our self-attachment and we hate what threatens it. Many of our more complex emotions are triggered in this way — resentment, jealousy, envy, spite, possessiveness, vengeance and so on.

The three poisons also get displaced into various specific pathologies. A fairly clear example is eating disorders. Compulsive eating is clearly a greed condition, but it also serves a number of self-building functions, making the person bigger so that they carry more weight while at the same time making them less sexually attractive thus avoiding what may be an area of difficulty. Anorexia is just as clearly a hate condition, but again it serves complex self-building and inter-personal functions, manipulating and punishing others as well as self. Bulimia is more directly in the province of delusion, being a love-hate activity in which the person is at war with him/herself. All these conditions include dimensions of refusal to really accept what it is to be an incarnate being living in a material world.

Delusion is conceit. It is what brings spiritual danger and leads us astray. In simple terms, this is pride. It may be clearly manifest or it may be hidden under all kinds of social strategies and dissimulation, but it is the root cause of our troubles.

Wavering Faith

Question: I clearly understand that I am saved by Amida through his name, but I do not experience this. Knowing cannot compare to feeling. Life is so easily lost, I fear death without certainty of my future. How can I make certain that I shall truly attain ojo*? If there is still doubt and I die next week, I have lived in vain.

Short answer: One cannot know. Shinran himself said, "I myself do not know that nembutsu is not the path to hell."

Longer Answer: We have doubt. We are bombu. It is our nature to be unsteady. Even Shinran said: "I myself do not know, after all, whether the nembutsu is truly the cause of our rebirth in the Pure Land or whether it is that karmic act that causes us to sink into bottomless hell." Shinran's faith is not built upon an achieved certainty about his salvation. It is based upon realisation that he is incapable of attaining nirvana by his own effort or virtue. Since he cannot reach salvation by his own power he has no choice but to rely upon other power and upon his teacher. Shinran also says that the very fact that we do not have ecstatic joy all the time when we think of the saving power

---

* Rebirth in the Pure Land

of nembutsu in our lives is itself evidence of our parlous condition and should be simply another thing that convinces us that we have to ask for help. The Pureland path definitely begins with reflection upon our own failings rather than with an attempt to accomplish perfect faith. When we make such a reflection we realise that we do not have the necessary self power to reach enlightenment by our own effort. Surprisingly, when we realise our own condition as hopeless cases, this knowledge is itself releasing. We realise that our salvation is simply not in our hands. Whether we really are spiritually secure or not is in the hands of the Buddha. When we realise this we can stop worrying about it. We just say the nembutsu and get on with what reality presents for us to do.

In the sutra it says that even one recitation of nembutsu is enough to connect one to Amitabha who will certainly take one to his Land, whether one believes it, understands it, or feels it, or not. Doubt is not a barrier. It is natural. There is no need to fear. All is completely assured.

Do Pureland Buddhists Practice Intercessory Prayer?

Question: I'm wondering how Pureland handles intercessory prayers. To whom do we pray to help others?

Short answer: No, we practise merit transference.

Longer answer: Intercessory prayer means asking a deity to deflect karmic consequence and so, from a Buddhist perspective, we would expect this to be ineffective since in the Buddhist view deities are as subject to karma as anybody else and karma is inexorable. However, Mahayana Buddhism at least does practice transference of merit. Transference of merit means that one claims no credit for one's own good acts. Since the merit attaching to an act is a function of several variables, one of the most important of which is the intention associated with the act, and since the credit we claim is a significant element in intentionality, the eschewal of credit renders the act unconditional in this respect and so multiplies the merit. Unconditional acts — i.e. acts for which merit is transferred — are thus particularly meritorious. Merit transfer, therefore, is the wish that whatever merit we may have go to the benefit of all beings, or, which amounts to the same thing, go toward the creation of a Pure Land.

Now merit transference may be universal or particular. In universal merit transference we wish that all beings benefit whereas in particular merit transference we wish that a specific being or group of beings benefit. The particularising of merit transference is really more a matter of orienting the practitioner and assisting him or her to think concretely about the afflictions in the world than anything else. If I make a prayer to transfer merit to all sentient beings, that is good. If I make a prayer to transfer merit to John Smith whom I know to be suffering from such and such an illness or if I pray to transfer merit to all the people caught up in such and such a famine or war, then I have to have thought concretely about the suffering of those people. That is the advantage of particular transference. On the other hand, in particular transference there is more scope for personal bias or egocentricity to tinge the act. We might be more inclined to transfer merit to those whom we believe to be on "our side", for instance. This is the disadvantage. Nonetheless, particularised merit transference does perform a role in Mahayana Buddhism that is quite similar to the role of intercessory prayer in a theistic religion.

In Pureland, there is the additional twist that the practitioner is in receipt of Amida's merit and so feels no need to accumulate personal merit. This reflection, in itself, is a profound practice. The Pureland practitioner does not really think that he or she has the power to direct merit, even though one might express a wish that such and such persons be helped. We believe, rather, that if we proceed in faith then grace will spread unimpededly.

Metta

Question: Other traditions talk a lot about generating metta for our friends, acquaintances and enemies. How would we talk about this in the Pureland tradition?

Short answer: Nembutsu is gratitude for Buddha's metta toward all beings.

Longer answer: The metta practice was originally given by Shakyamuni to some young Brahmins who wanted to know how to dwell closer to Brahma. He taught them to suffuse the four directions with "An awareness imbued with goodwill." In Pureland, our basic practice is awareness of the goodwill of all the Buddhas, and especially Amitabha Buddha. We imagine that Buddha is continuously benefitting all beings in all directions. Those beings might or might not be appreciating such blessings, but the Dharma rain is still continuously falling, as it says in the Lotus Sutra Parable of the Herbs. If we are Pureland Buddhists, we are likely to be happy about that. Furthermore, the light of Buddha is reflected in those beings and we ourselves are thus benefitted. So we are grateful for that too.

"Love is already in the world."

It is not we ourselves who are going to create love. Love is already in the world. As long as we do not get in the way, it reflects in us perfectly, and when we do get in the way, then it still reflects in us, if imperfectly. Actually, real love is, therefore, perfect inner stillness. To love is to not manipulate. Buddhas are like that. We, of course, are just ordinary beings so we are rarely so still. Often enough we are in a fever of fear or desire, but if we put our attention on the Buddha we will realise that he is rather good at calming us down. The Buddha light is radiant in all directions, supporting all beings each in their appropriate way. Knowing this can help us to relax at a deeper level and not be so frightened anymore, because we do not need to take responsibility for everything. If we allow the Buddhas to do their work, and not try to do it for them, we can live in happiness and our practice, whatever it may be, will then be a ritual of gratitude and appreciation.

Personal Practice verses Relationship

Question: Both meditation and modern (and post-modern) psychotherapy focus on the 'ego' (or 'non-ego') or 'self' (or 'non-self'). There is great merit in this but, in my view, it is not the direction of future development in meditation and psychotherapy. Focus on the self (or non-self) has reached a plateau in both fields. In 1979, Trevarthen discovered "primary intersubjectivity," the fact that infants accurately estimate the subjectivity of their mothers. This discovery is to psychology as the Michelson-Morley experiment was to physics because it presents facts that cannot be explained by modern psychology. And traditional meditation theory has been silent about the nature and development of the intersubjective even though Vajrayana Buddhism and Tantric Hinduism make extensive reference to it. The new focus, I predict, will be on the intersubjective or interpersonal.

Short answer: Yes, practice is an encounter with Buddha, with Sangha, and with the world as it is.

Longer answer: Thank you. Broadly, I agree. The interpretation of Buddhism that one finds in the Pureland tradition, certainly the way we practise it at Amida Shu, is inter-subjective and other-oriented. Our interpretation of non-self, anatma, is that it means "other" and this is supported by philological analysis.

The challenge lies in the difficulty of understanding inter-subjectivity. Simply saying that people have equal rights, for instance, is insufficient since rights is a legal rather than a psychological or spiritual concept, but there is a need for people to reach a state in which they are able to tolerate spiritual equality and this means having a deep sense of being the recipient of love that can survive transient periods when there is abundant evidence of its absence, not merely an intention to do good, though such intention is also important. In practice in any given interaction there are inherent imbalances and maturity requires an ability to navigate these without getting capsized. While studies of infants are, of course, enormously useful, I would resist the idea that knowing about infants always and necessarily tells us about adults. Infants and adults both are dependent upon ambient conditions.

That meditation does not equip people for inter-personal relationships is broadly true — in fact it can make people self-preoccupied and, in the worst cases, actually be destructive of relationships. On the other hand, there are different kinds of meditation. In the Pureland tradition, the Buddhist practice of dhyana that has traditionally been divided into the categories of vipashyana (quan) and shamatha (chih) has taken form as nei quan (or naikan) and chih quan which are spiritual exercises that both (especially the former) have reflection upon interpersonal events as a focus.

Another major factor in inter-subjectivity is shame and this has been a rather taboo subject in psychology for a long time. I agree that we could do with more studies of how people modulate the vicissitudes of acceptance and rejection that go on in all relationships. Progress toward inter-subjective maturity would seem, in general, to require opportunities to participate in inter-personal arenas that are relatively safe, but still challenging, coupled with opportunity for and encouragement toward detailed reflection upon experience. It is important that such reflection itself occur in an ambiance in which the major issues are not pre-judged and this condition is more difficult to meet than one might at first assume since our culture is shot through with innumerable taboos and ideals on this matter. Thank you.

No 'How to' in Nirvana

Question: How can one enter Nirvana, if to do so is to extinguish all craving, and if to love is entwined in craving? Or isn't it? But I can't see how it isn't.

Short answer: Our love involves desire. We are what we are: that is nirvana enough.

Longer answer: We sometimes intuit 'unconditional love' and that intuition is itself an ecstasy because it is knowledge of what we are not. We ourselves are conditioned and conditional beings. Consequently, there is no 'how' to entering nirvana. Nirvana is not part of a sequence in time nor result of a cause. To know nirvana is a grace, a gift that comes to us sometimes, but we cannot have the receiving of such a gift under our control. Were we to do so it would no longer be the gift. In fact, it appears spontaneously when self becomes dark, but self cannot darken itself — any attempt to do so is a pose.

People tend to interpret Buddhism as a technical model: if you do this and this then that will happen. I don't interpret it that way. To me, the things that are slated as 'steps toward' are actually consequences. The Eightfold Path did not get Buddha enlightened. He discovered the Eightfold Path as a result of being enlightened. If nirvana touches your life you may be inspired to love more, but if you try to love more "in order to" touch nirvana you will fail. Paradoxically, it is when you fail that nirvana may touch you, but it is in the nature of things that you can never have guarantees, or be in control of this. One cannot plan to fail.

> *"Nirvana is without strife, yet Buddha said that a day without striving is a wasted day."*

A mother loves her child. This is, perhaps, as near to unconditional as it gets for us mortals. But the unconditional part of this love is very deep. At a day to day level, the mother may lose her temper with the child and the mother seeks various satisfactions in the child. There is a power struggle between the growing child and the parent and if the child is unable to defeat the parent's ego in this struggle, it will not thrive. Even in this quasi-unconditional love there has to be struggle, victory and defeat.

Nirvana, on the other hand, is complete peace. Can I be at peace with the fact that I am at war? This is the paradox of a real spiritual life. Nirvana is without strife, yet Buddha said that a day without striving is a wasted day. Our nirvana is to be in samsara, inspired by our fragmentary intuition of nirvana.

Buddha had no method for becoming enlightened and all the teachings that various schools offer on the basis of the idea that he did are mistaken. Neither sitting still, nor doing good deeds, nor controlling the mind, nor anything else he chose to do caused Buddha to be enlightened. He was enlightened when, being totally defeated, he was nonetheless helped and then blessed by the sight of the natural beauty of the morning star rising.

Experiencing Universal Love

Question: While I have been chanting Namo Amida Bu, on a daily basis, for three years, just last week I received some insights. In my experience and process I recognized three stages:

1. **Calling out to Amida**
   Having faith about other power, Amida — trusting and finding a safe space. Feeling at ease when my mind goes crazy. When having nightmares I call out to Amida and feel safe again.
2. **Receiving**
   Just last week when I did my nembutsu, suddenly and very unexpected I received love. When I call out I feel love, being held. The Light of Amida is shining on me and in me.
3. **Giving**
   Then a miracle happened. Just after stage 2. Calling out to Amida I recognized that I am love. I am giving love. Light pours out of me. Calling out to Amida is giving love to the world.

Is this something you recognize and/or can comment on?

Short answer: Such experiences are a grace. Do not cling to them, but be grateful.

Longer answer: Yes, thank you. Excellent. This kind of experience is most likely to happen when one is a bit separated from one's normal everyday routine. When we create a kind of safe space away from our everyday stimuli it is easier for Amida to reach us. Even if we are at home it helps if we create a space with some boundaries (even a quarter hour in a special place). This is similar to therapy, there has to be a safe space. Simply having faith is a way of creating such a space and if one has enough faith one has such a space wherever one is.

Then within that space, if there is an open heart, light may enter. Then occasionally one maybe has such an experience. This experience will fade, but it will never go away completely. It will remain like a candle burning in the depths of the cave of one's mind and it will give one strength in the future, helping one to make wiser decisions and to cope with set-backs without despair. It is a glimpse of how life would be if one were free from one's "ordinary neurosis". We all suffer from a variety of ordinary neuroses that give us stress and bad dreams and impede our daily life, but we also have intermittent access to the sacred light which is liberation.

"From time to time, the angels will touch you."

Occasionally, usually when we are in retreat of some kind, the neurosis temporarily drops away or is over-whelmed by the light. This glimpse is precious. We cannot demand that the light come back, but our nembutsu is a reminder of it and an expression of gratitude for it and this helps us to remain open.

The more we remain open to this light, the more it appears in our life. The angels speak to us if we go on listening. This is really the root of all creativity. Different people will talk about it in different ways. Amida communicates in whatever way might work for the particular person. After we have had such experience we return to ordinary life. We cannot hang onto the experience, but it remains an important landmark that we can refer back to in our mind. It strengthens our faith and helps us in life. Our ordinary neurosis continues, but, as it were, alongside it, there is now another thread.

Recognising stages in the process is fine, but do not then think that this is some kind of formula that can be repeated. We cannot coerce Amida in any way. In fact, it is a major element in having faith that one realise this. No procedure or routine will make Amida behave the way we want. One has to let go of that element of self power. Just live your life. Enjoy; play; create; help and be helped; and, from time to time, the angels will touch you.

Even Good People go to the Pure Land

Question: There is a quote attributed to Shinran that says something like "Even the good person attains birth in the Pure Land, how much more so the evil person"....I'm finding this statement difficult to understand, perhaps you could offer an explanation

Short answer: Amida Buddha's Pure Land is primarily for the non-good, i.e. for people like us, but good people are not excluded.

Longer answer: Thank you. This quotation comes from Tannisho which is a work compiled by Shinran's disciple Yuien after the master's death. The first half consists entirely of quotations from Shinran and this is one of them. It brings out Shinran's distinctive take on what Buddhism, especially Pureland Buddhism, is all about. Essentially there are two possible approaches to Buddhism. One approach is to become a Buddha oneself by one's own effort by achieving moral perfection, meditative stability and limitless wisdom. That approach is called the Path for Sages. The other approach is to rely upon the Buddha's grace. In this second approach one is transformed naturally by allowing the Buddha to enter one's life. This is a path of faith and ecstatic response to the Tathagatha's transcendent presence. This latter is called

Pureland. It is the bhaktiyoga of Buddhism where the Path of Sages is the rajayoga. Teachers like Honen and Shinran observed that although the Sages Path was the official form of Buddhism in their day, the so called sages did not exemplify the standards established in the sutras. In fact, nobody exemplifies them. Some people are better than others, but nobody actually matches the level of perfection supposedly required. They concluded that we must now be in mappo, the Dharma-ending age, when nobody has the capacity to follow the Sage Path completely any more. So Pureland rests on the principle that there are two approaches to Buddhism in principle, but only one works in practice. The one that works is the Pureland Path and that is what Honen taught.

> "This makes Pureland, in one sense, the most simple, basic form of religion there is."

Now the Pureland path is specifically the method for bombu, i.e. ordinary people who do not have super-human capacities for moral perfection, meditative stability, or limitless wisdom. We bombu cannot get to nirvana by effort and self-refinement, only by relying upon the fact that Buddha - especially Amida Buddha — accepts us as we are (rather than as we would be if we perfected ourselves). Entering the Pure Land is, therefore, for bombu, not for the virtuous. But since Amida's compassion is without limit, one must say that even virtuous people are also allowed. Hence, even the virtuous enter the Pureland, how much more so sinners.

What this means is that Pureland or Amidism is religion for ordinary people — for Mr and Mrs Everybody. In Pureland we make the simple basic religious distinction between the sacred and the mundane. The mundane is ourselves and our world. The sacred is Amida and the Pure Land. Our religious practice then consists of the feelings we have when we contemplate this configuration and we express these feelings by calling the Buddha's name, usually in the form "Namo Amida Bu." This call is called the nembutsu. It may express longing, joy, despair, gratitude, awe, request, hope, excitement, calm — the whole range of religious sentiment. It gathers into one phrase the whole expression of our reflection upon our own short-coming in relation to the sacred realm that we contemplate and call upon. It is only meaningful, however, in relation to a sincere and deep realisation that we are bombu and the Buddha is not.

This makes Pureland, in one sense, the most simple, basic form of religion there is — simple enough for bombu like us. However, there is also a subtlety in it, since Shinran is aware that the person who strives toward self-perfection is also the person who does not really have faith in anything other than themselves and such a person actually has much more difficulty entering into the grace that religion offers. Such a person is really trying to stay in control of their own fate and has not got the basic willingness to trust what religion is all about. So this more subtle sense is a second dimension of meaning in what Shinran is saying. An everyday illustration of this spiritual problem is found in the fact that we can commonly observe that people who are ethically strict are often, by the same token, intolerant, whereas there are plenty of examples of people who are self-indulgent who are equally happy to indulge others and so are more tolerant and easier to live with even though they perhaps keep their precepts less strictly. Virtue does not always make for heaven, either for oneself or others.

Amidism is, therefore, that most basic form of religion in which unholy beings such as we contemplate holy things; and do so in such a way that feelings arise in us — feelings that then reshape our life, death, sense of our place in the universe, and so on. It is about naturalness and fellow-feeling rather than perfectionism. Shinran had this special talent for one-liners that bring this situation home to us with immediacy.

Precepts or Not?

Question: Some say that if you have faith there is no need for precepts and some say that the attempt to keep precepts is a self power practice and therefore not appropriate to Pureland. What is your view on this?

Short answer: If you have faith, then the behaviour that precepts recommend comes naturally.

Longer answer: Strictly speaking it is true in principle that faith removes the need for precepts, but not in the manner that this assertion is often understood. Precepts simply describe the life of a person of deep faith. This is another example of how what is commonly taken as a means is actually an outcome.

People like Shan Tao and Honen were men of deep faith and so their lives conformed to the precepts. If a person has strong faith then they are likely to live in the manner described by the precepts so if you have faith the important things will take care of themselves. If a person claims to have faith, but does not live according to the precepts, or if a person claims to have had an awakening of faith and their behaviour has not changed in this direction, then their claim to faith may be suspect. At the same time, however, there may be reasons why a person of faith might, or might not be able to keep certain precepts. A bodhisattva may have to adopt a particular lifestyle in order to reach some people who would otherwise be completely lost. One might see Shinran's life in this light. Or a person may be trapped in conditions that make it impossible to keep the precepts. The warrior and the prostitute encountered by Honen Shonin on his way into exile would be examples. Or again a person's psychological make-up may be so dominated by unfortunate karma that he or she does not have sufficient control to keep certain precepts. One should therefore hesitate to pass judgement upon another person since the depth of another's heart is always hidden from us.

Precepts are useful to us because they give us a measure upon our faith and they highlight our bombu nature to us. Precepts can be a valuable basis as nei quan exercises. Through examining ourselves in the light of the precepts we gain a deep sense of our nature and this enriches our devotion. Again it is important to consider the precepts from the collective rather than merely the individual point of view. The precepts kept by one person are a support to the faith of others and those who break the precepts without good cause undermine the faith of others. It is very clear that Nyorai gave us these precepts and wants us to keep them as part of his scheme to save all sentient beings. We therefore do the best we can while recognising our bombu nature. Honen Shonin administered the precepts and did his best to keep them and those of us who have ordained or taken precepts all do likewise.

In relation to your question as put, it may also be useful to ask, necessary for what? Necessary for personal salvation? for keeping order in society? for making oneself pure? — to ask if this or that is necessary in this context seems to imply, is it necessary in order that one get... However, such a gaining idea is probably more of a distraction than a help.

Practising while Sinning

Question: Honen Shonin taught us that no matter what one may be doing, do it with the nembutsu. But at times I realize I am doing things that are not in accord with the Buddha way, at such times I feel it wrong to think of Amida. So the thought has come to me that I should try to keep precepts, so I can always recite nembutsu. Do you think it is OK to recite, even though one is in the act of sinning? Or can one see the precepts as an accessory to nembutsu?

Short answer: Thank you for your very good question. It is good to say nembutsu in all conditions, so there is no need to worry.

Longer answer:

1. It is always an inherently good thing to keep the precepts. This is just a matter of definition — the precepts are a description of what is good to do. The precepts indicate the kind of life that Buddha wants one to live: the kind that does not generate suffering for oneself or others. It is, therefore, good to act in accordance with the precepts.

2. At the same time as Honen encourages us to keep the precepts he also points out that we are not good at doing so. We often fail. The efficacy of saying the nembutsu is not, however, dependent upon one's virtue. One should say the nembutsu whether one is being virtuous or not. In fact, it is precisely by realising how we depart far from the precepts that makes us realise that we need the nembutsu.

> *"I am one of Amida's people, already in receipt of Amida's grace, in due course to be refreshed in the Pure Land, meanwhile to assist in Amida's work of transformation, and ultimately take on the role of a Buddha".*

3. Keeping the precepts is, however, broadly indicative of one's state of faith. To break a precept is generally an instance of 'short-term-ism'. One breaks the precept in order to get a quick benefit even though one knows that in the longer run one generates trouble. To not do so requires faith in the longer run process of life and this, for a Pureland person, is a reflection of one's faith in Amida. If I am confident that I am one of Amida's people, already in receipt of Amida's grace, in due course to be refreshed in the Pure Land, meanwhile to assist in Amida's work of transformation, and ultimately take on the role of a Buddha, then there is no need for me to break precepts. To steal or lie or cheat or be greedy, etc., will have no appeal if my faith is in my commitment to a purpose that will be hindered by all such acts. It is not so much that the precepts are restrictions as that one is so intent on the path of faith that sins just seem like distractions from what one really wants to do.

4. The precepts, therefore, are not so much an accessory to nembutsu as a natural extension of it. If I realise that I have broken them it is an indicator to myself that my faith was somewhere else at that time. It gives some insight into my bombu condition and the karma that I consist of. I may feel contrite. I should certainly say the nembutsu.

5. If I place my faith in the nembutsu and take refuge in the Buddhas rather than in worldly gain, then the motivation to break the precepts will be undermined by degrees and naturally I shall live a more virtuous life, simply because I will be conscious of the disadvantage of doing otherwise. This process of undermining goes on largely unconsciously, however. It is like the person who falls in love. They then no longer want to do things that will impede their relation with the beloved — not because they are making a big effort so much as because it would run counter to their aim in life. Sometimes old habits may still prevail, but when they do the person feels anguish at himself. That is exactly the time when the person is likely to reflect upon the name of the beloved.

What Happens When an Amidist Dies?

Question: What can an Amidist expect in the period immediately following death? Is there anything written on that by Shinran, Honen etc? How does it compare for instance to the bardo experience described in the Tibetan Book of Living and Dying?

Short answer: He or she goes directly to the Pure Land.

Longer answer: In the Larger Pureland Sutra it says that a person who has had strong faith and lived accordingly will be met by Amida Buddha and taken directly to the Pure Land without any intervening bardo state. A person of medium faith will see a vision of Amida Buddha and will also be born directly into the Pure Land. A person of slight faith will see Amida as if in a dream and will be reborn in the Pure Land. Within the Pure Land all must continue to experience the effects of past karma but the environment is such that it is much easier to work through these effects. Also, there are two kinds of career within the Pure Land. Ordinary disciples (shravakas) enjoy the Pure Land for a very long time and then eventually when the issues arising from their karma are all cleared up, enter nirvana.

Bodhisattvas, however, clear up such issues much quicker, but do not enter nirvana. Instead they return to this world or other worlds like this one to continue the work of liberation and transformation.

Other Lives

Question: What is your take on the afterlife?

Short answer: I'm looking forward to it.

Longer answer: My sense of this is based principally upon my own memory of having had the kind of experiences that people call visionary both as a child and, during intense spiritual practice and occasionally other times, as an adult. This has left me in the position where, if I believe my experience rather than my education, it appears to me that there are other lives before and after this one and there are realms of light or great radiance where one might be reborn or have spent time in the past. My Buddhist beliefs concur with these experiences and add that none of these resting places is permanent. They also add theories about karma which suggest that one's destiny in one life is a function of one's wilful behaviour or state of mind in previous ones. However, if there are many lives in this way, the complexity of one's karma must be so astronomical that this probably does not help a lot as far as prediction might go.

Where this leaves me, in terms of how such belief may affect this life is that since the powers in the universe may take us to all manner of destinies including some beyond our current imagination, what matters is primarily to live in a state of faith and willingness, open to whatever comes. Such faith and willingness is, in my thinking, closely allied with love, both the sense of being loved and the need to love. We are wandering through many lives longing to love as completely as possible, meeting with many obstacles, frustrations and disappointments, yet endlessly recharged by the love that we receive, whether we acknowledge it or not. This perspective is not entirely orthodox for Buddhism — it is my own attempt to make sense of my own experience with a bit of help from the tradition.

Love thus implies equanimity. One does not love for a motive or for attachment to a goal. Love takes all in its stride. What will happen to me in my next life? I do not know, but I am willing. I am willing to enter it in a loving spirit. If it is, indeed, direct rebirth in the Sukhavati of Amitabha Buddha I shall rejoice at such good fortune, but if the Buddhas have other work for me to do I shall rejoice that I am needed for its accomplishment. I do not need to know in advance exactly what will befall. When I have had near-death experiences there has been a strong sense that dying leads somewhere and that the transition is of immense importance and at those times I felt willing. I somehow knew that whatever I needed to know in order to do what was necessary would be provided to me at the time. Perhaps because of such experience, I now have relatively little need to be in control. Travelling the world to teach Dharma, I put myself in other people's hands. I take on situations that are unfamiliar. I do not plan over-much; just the minimum necessary to be responsible. It is as though every situation is a new life. When the time comes for me to die I expect it will be the same.

What is Buddha?

Question: Recently I have been pondering the question: "What is Buddha?" For it seems that once we jump into Pureland Buddhism we are in the realm of the "Cosmic Buddha." Elsewhere, Amida is defined as meaning "without measure" as the Buddha of limitless light. This seems clear enough and yet I am wondering how or even if this differs from the Christian God or the Hindu God or the Islamic God or the Taoist Tao? Is Amida the Buddhist God? What are your thoughts?

Short answer: Buddha is our spiritual friend.

Longer answer: Big subject — here are some part answers:

1. The question "What is Buddha?" has a lot in it and it is probably not much of an over-statement to say that it was reflection upon this and related questions that gave birth to the whole of Mahayana Buddhism. Given that Siddhatha Gotama died a long time ago, what is one taking refuge in when one takes refuge in Buddha? Buddhists clearly have a sense that Buddha is not just dead and gone.

2. The term "cosmic Buddha" usually refers to Vairochana. Vairochana is considered the embodiment of Dharmakaya. Simplistically we can equate:

a. Vairochana — Dharmakaya
b. Amida — Sambhogakaya
c. Shakyamuni — Nirmanakaya

but this does not always work as some sages talk about three kaya Amidas and in any case there are many, many Buddhas and, in princple, all have all three aspects, but this does mean that, as we generally encounter him, Amida is not the ultimate abstraction of Buddhahood, so much as the most exalted aspect that we corporeal beings can experience or encounter in our current state.

3. As for the comparison with the theistic god:

Similarities:
Amida saves,
Amida is light, love, wisdom
Amida is object of devotion

Differences:
Amida did not create the world
Amida does not judge
Amida does not answer personal prayers

4. The tone of Amidism is quite different to the tone of theism. We are traveling in North America at the time of writing this[*] and here there is a lot of debate on the question, how can you believe in an all good omnipotent creator god after the tsunami? Well, this just does not arise in Buddhism. Tsunamis are made by nature, not by Amida — he/she/it is as subject to them as we are. We are dependent, weak beings. We need help. Amida helps. Amida is not fundamentally on a different plane from ourselves.

Question 2: Thank you for your insightful reply. There is some question nagging my mind but I cannot find the words to articulate it. Yes, we do get to skip over the whole problem of Theodicy. I particularly appreciate your concise comparison of Amida with the theistic creator god. I never thought of "Buddha" as something that I would have a personal relationship with. I guess it was just very abstract. Buddha was either historical or mythological for me. Buddha is a title that means awake or awakening. So when I take refuge in Buddha I am taking refuge in Awakening. Amida means limitless. So when I take refuge in Amida Buddha I am taking refuge in limitless Awakening. This seems very clear. After all, I am always limiting reality with my misperceptions and clinging to self. Limitlessness seems a very positive way to articulate non-self.

If at every moment I try to awaken to the limitless nature of reality then I begin to perceive the world from outside the crushing wheel of samsara. But where does the bhakti

---

[*] 2004

element of Amidism come from? One of my core practices is a Pureland practice, but it is not particularly devotional for my part. It feels more like a constant retraining in how to perceive and think about the world. Is Amida just our vocabulary for awakening and Amidism just our methodology or our upaya for attaining Awakening? When we encounter Buddhists from other traditions can we just change our vocabulary a little? Instead of talking about Amida when hanging out in Zen circles we talk about emptiness. When we are in the Tibetan Gompa we talk about Guru Yoga and Mahamudra or Rigpa. When we are with Theravadins we talk about non-self. I apologize for the lack of clarity! I hope that someone can intuit what thread I am pulling at and shed some light.

Answer: Not everybody's religious feeling or mystical experience is the same. Perhaps there is an ultimate reconciliation, but we do not live in the ultimate dimension, we live in the existential world. Religious feeling and mystical experience occur to beings like us, here in the relative world. Sometimes the form they take is abstract, sometimes personal. Rigpa refers to the experience of pure spiritual light. Amida is such light, so rigpa is Amida. However, Amida also appears to us as a person. In the Tibetan system this is not called rigpa, this is called yidam. It is therefore possible to have a personal relation with Amida, or with one's yidam, but the idea of having a personal relationship with rigpa does not make a lot of sense. Amida could appear to us as anything, according to the sensitivity of the particular person. Many people experience the light of Amida reflected in their experience of the natural world.

> *"I understand our Pureland religion not so much as a body of doctrine, but more as a way of working with religious feeling."*

Because Amida is mostly thought of as sambhogakaya, we are not thinking of something absolute and ultimate — a oneness within which all opposites are finally reconciled — we are talking about the kind of spiritual experience that ordinary foolish beings like ourselves do sometimes have. Such experience is relative in that it has characteristics that can be expressed in dualistic language — it impresses us in particular ways that are different from other possibilities — perhaps making us feel inspired rather than dejected, say. It may take the form of a dream or a vision or an altered state of consciousness, for instance. None of these is formless nor ultimate but they are beyond the normal.

If you want to tell Amida what you are doing in your life, you can and Amida may give you signs that guide you, but we do not usually think of Amida answering direct petitionary prayer. Amida does not manipulate this world — he/she/it helps us to awaken faith and become free from existential anxiety. It would not be appropriate to pray to Amida for a better job or that Aunt Jane not die just yet, but one might experience Amida's blessing and guidance, and that might be very personal and specific. You might experience in a dream or a sudden intuition exactly what Aunt Jane needs in order to die well.

The bhakti in Buddhism no doubt derives directly from the feelings people had about the sage Gotama. There was something about that man that made him more than just an ordinary being, even though, in a slightly different sense, that "something" could be said to reside in the fact that he was the most ordinary being who ever walked the earth. Such "thusness", however, was deeply cherished by all who followed him. Thus it is easy to envisage the origin of devotion that is sometimes directed toward the person and sometimes toward the quality abstracted, as it were, from the example of that special person's life, work and way of being. I understand our Pureland religion not so much as a body of doctrine, but more as a way of working with religious feeling. There are doctrines, for sure, but they exist just to provide a holding framework within which we can express and explore our faith in and love for the Tathagata. Faith does not manifest as one constant mind state. It wheels through many modes. Sometimes there is the ecstasy of shinjin experience; sometimes the quiet confidence we call anjin; sometimes the spiritual intimacy called shimmitsu; sometimes the purposefulness of bodaishin (bodhichitta). Sometimes it takes the form of a clear conceptual understanding; sometimes a vision of light; sometimes a personal encounter. Amida is all of these things, appearing according to the need, phase and capacity of the particular person of faith.

> *"One does still find groups of Buddhists with tambourines and drums who sing themselves into Buddha bhakti."*

These days, bhakti is associated more with Hindism and especially groups like Hare Krishna. They sing themselves into a trance of devotion to their god. While I was in Assam, however, I discovered that this Hindu bhakti practice has actually been taken over from Buddhism. It seems that what has happened is that Buddhism has become somewhat puritanical and lost some of its devotional fervour and this narrowness led to people converting to Hinduism which at that time was lax and diverse, where they could go on singing, dancing and getting high on devotion, as they still do to this day. I think that we need to reincorporate this lost aspect of Buddhism and not be so tight. One does still find groups of Buddhists with tambourines and drums who sing themselves into Buddha bhakti and if one looks at the original text of many Buddhist scriptures they are written in rhythmic poetry, probably intended originally to be sung. Translating into plain prose in English we lose all that, but that may be the important part.

As for changing terminology when with other groups, all these sets of terms make sense in the context of Buddhism as a whole and there are some equivalences and sometimes it takes some sorting out to know what goes with what. I think we can assume that they are all ways of talking about the same thing ultimately, but the emphasis tends to be different from school to school. The differences between Buddhist schools are not, for the most part, doctrinal, they are simply differences of emphasis. We all study, we all have devotions, we all have writings on morality, we all do spiritual exercises, we all respect our teachers and we all take refuge in Buddha — just some put more emphasis on one aspect and some on another and over the centuries, out of the vast wealth of Buddhist literature, different groups have favoured different texts. This gives an appearance of greater difference than is in fact the case.

> Budd-ham sara-nam gac-chami
> Dhar-mam sara-nam gac-chami
> Sang-ham sara-nam gac-chami
> The heady night fills
> until even the birds
> are siging the Dharma.

How Should I Regard Amida?

Question: I'm a recent, enthusiastic convert to Shin and have read through your insightful and thought-provoking posts on your website as well as reading all the Shin literature I can find on the web. So much of it speaks very deeply to me. But I remain confused and conflicted about a central issue that even seems to divide Shin followers — how to view the "reality" of Amida. Some seem to view Amida as having some form of personhood, others seem to see Amida as only symbolic. Frankly, I'm torn, coming from a nominally Zen background inclining me to see Amida as merely symbolic of True Mind, yet I find it difficult to muster adequate devotion to a mere symbol. This was a topic I did not see you address on your site and would dearly love to have some guidance from your perspective. Your writings have been very inspirational to me and actually tipped the scales for me to become a Shin convert. So thank you so much for your work.

Short answer: Amida is a real person and is a Buddha Tathagata.

Longer answer: Thank you for this question. You are quite right that you will find a range of interpretations among Shin and Pureland practitioners and in the literature. I myself have explored a number of possibilities in my gradual penetration into these teachings. It is a common modern trend to psychologise or spiritualise teachings in a manner that takes the stuffing out of them. There seem to me to be only two credible ways of interpreting, say, the Larger Pureland Sutra and the difference between them hinges on what you think Shakyamuni was doing in his dialogue with Ananda. Either Shakyamuni is telling an allegory or he is telling a history. If it is an allegory, then Amida is simply a symbolic character in a story and the story is probably meant actually to tell us something about Shakyamuni himself. If the story is history then we are being given a cosmological vision and being told something about the greater process that is going on. I'm going to opt for the latter.

First, however, let's deal with a few subsidiary points. Firstly, neither Amida nor the Pure Land are symbols for a state of mind since faith in Amida must persist through changes in mind state. One can have shinjin while in a wide range of different states of mind.

Secondly, neither Amida nor the Pure Land can be "inside us" either in the sense of being our "Buddha nature" or our "true mind" or our "real self" or any other of these rather dubious solipsistic metaphysical concepts that have become widespread, since the whole point is that Amida creates a land that we can inhabit. If we can be in the Pure Land, then the Pure Land is not in us. We might belong to the Pure Land or relate to Amida, but it is essential to the whole scheme of religious ideas in Amida Buddhism that we are saved by a power that is "other". In this sense, Amidism is a natural conclusion of the doctrine of non-self — salvation is other (sarva dharma anatma

— all Dharma is not self) and we simply do not have the power to save ourselves.

Thirdly, Amida wants to save us and Amida loves us as we are — not as super-refined spirit entities, but in the flesh. This means inter alia that Amida is a sentient being who accepts us as sentient beings.

Fourthly, Amida comes to us as a saviour, which means that Amida is a Tathagata in the sense of Tatha-agata or Nyorai — one who comes from Tatha to us. We do not have to work our passage to him — he comes to us.

Fifthly, the Pure Land is "in the West" meaning that it is not "on high", therefore, Amida is a beneficent sentient being who is not a god. This means that Amida is some kind of real person. And what a one!

Now modern people such as ourselves are not probably going to take it that the Pure Land is a place in the West in a literal sense. I suggest above that "in the West" basically means "on our level", i.e. human-type not god-type. Also, there will be doubts about the chronology that puts Amida's enlightenment sometime several Big Bangs ago. Presumably, therefore, Shakyamuni is talking about something timeless rather than epochal. This is also what the name Amitayus would imply.

> *"We have to entrust ourselves to something and at that point nothing meagre is going to do."*

What we have therefore is that a bodhisattva (Dharmakara) through the inspiration (other power) of a Buddha (Lokeshvararaja) gives rise to great altruistic intention (the vows) and works to generate a paradise (Sukhavati) where all who enter may have ideal conditions for awakening. This is the story of Amida, but it is also prototypical for all Buddhas. There are many Buddhas. All have an essentially similar career. Exactly what the geography and chronology of all this is defy human understanding, but Shakyamuni gives us a picture right on the edge of human scale imagination in order to indicate that the reality is out of our frame. Nonetheless, it is a model. One day, if we sustain our faith, you and I shall generate such Pure Lands and welcome myriads of beings. That day may be several big bangs into the future — who knows?

This is therefore not a story that can be reduced to human scale or naturalistic proportions and thereby be explained away. It remains as a basis of our faith, a framework within which our lives as they actually are (not as they might be after spiritual refinement) become meaningful. When we have exhausted the limits of prajna wisdom and no longer have any worldly ground to stand on we have to entrust ourselves to something and at that point nothing meagre is going to do. Shakyamuni says entrust yourself to Amida and Amida will save you. Amida is not a mere symbol. Amida is a real person who is a Buddha Tathagata who will really take you to the Pure Land. You and I do not fully comprehend what the Pure Land is, nor how he does it, but then we don't understand death or life either, nor the limits of space nor the nature of time or eternity, but we intuit them and, if we are not too steeped in cynicism, we also intuit the grandeur of Shakyamuni's teaching in the Pure Land Sutras.

We can entrust to Shakyamuni's words or not — that's up to us. If we do entrust to them, then we take Amida to be a real Buddha who has the power to take us to a pure domain at the time of our death no matter our state. This last is the crucial point since in Pureland Buddhism salvation is not a function of attaining a moral condition, a state of mind, a proficiency in spiritual practice, a social or institutional standing, or anything of that kind. Amida loves us just as we are. As Shakyamuni says in the (Pali) Snake Simile Sutta, "All who love me, all who believe in me, are all headed for heaven." To have faith in one Buddha is to have faith in all Buddhas.

In the meantime, Amida's light shines for us. All Buddha Tathagatas are engaged in a great work of transformation. The Pure Land Sutras set out a vision of Sukhavati which is not just a vision for one far away domain, but for all Buddha Lands. As Pureland Buddhists we are all carried along in the work of creating mini-replica Pure Lands wherever we may be. Just like refugees, once we know our true home and ultimate destination, we naturally start replicating it locally. Pureland thus also gives us a frame for engaged Buddhism that is rooted directly in our own scriptures and is not a case of Western liberal thinking added on to Buddhist sensibility, but rather a direct application of our own principles. The Pureland Buddhist does not worry about his or her own salvation. We do not need to do endless hours of self-salvific practice. We are therefore free to get on with the Buddha's work which is not self-serving. In essence it is a very simple faith that gives us an ability to have fellow feeling both for all people of faith no matter their creed and also for all manner of folk no matter their virtue, intelligence or affiliation. That's something.

Amida Buddhism is thus engaged, visionary, faith based, devotional, egalitarian, altruistic, inclusive, tolerant, confident, and mystical all at the same time. Stick with it.

Awaiting your coming
I sing your song
Amida Buddha
come along, come along,
into your hands I gladly fall
take me, take me, beyond the all.

Adhisthana

Question: Can you explain the notion of adhisthana, its relation to guru-yoga in Tibetan Mahayana, and say whether this is the same or different from Amidist Pureland?

Short answer: Adhisthana is another Mahayana term for other power.

Longer answer: Adhisthana refers to spiritual support. It is that upon which one can take one's stand. It is a reliable condition as opposed to worldly conditions that are subject to impermanence. Adhisthana is not subject to impermanence because it is not itself dependent upon anything. Hence the notion of shunyata. Adhisthana is, therefore, other power (Chinese ta-li, Japanese ta riki) and it is the Pure Land (Jing tu, Jodo). Do not think that other power and the land are two separate things, any more than the laws of physics and the physical world are different things. To rely upon one is to rely on the other.

This is all linked up with the teaching of dependent origination. We are dependently originated beings (fragile, vulnerable, fallible, impermanent), but what can we take refuge in? Adhisthana is refuge and refuge-power.

In Buddhism, adhisthana is what Buddhas rely upon. Buddhas share it with Buddhas. Since the disciple regards the teacher as a Buddha, for the disciple adhisthana resides with the teacher and, hence, with the lineage of teachers. However, it is also recognised that teachers may have found adhisthana directly from an encounter with a cosmic Buddha such as Amida Nyorai or by remembering his land. This would be the case, for instance, with Honen who had his awakening on reading Shan Tao's Commentary.

If, at any time in the vast wanderings of time, one has ever chanced upon that land of light then all that is necessary is that one remember. Anything may be sufficient to awaken such a memory. Such remembering is an-amnesia (smriti). Real "mindfulness" is anamnesia. You will find interesting things written about this in Plato, too.

Actually, it is my impression that this is common and this is, substantially, the Pureland position. A teacher may point out the Buddha, but we are all standing in the same position in relation to Him and, as soon as we realise it we also realise that we stand on the adhisthana just as He does.

> *"Guru power is a sub-set of lineage power and lineage power is a sub-set of other power."*

In my own case, I had powerful spiritual awakening long before I knew anything about Buddhism. Later, when I met teachers I had more experiences that they recognised and that I recognised as being the same in essence as the earlier ones. This is quite common. Many people have awakening experiences and so enter the path. They are not all signed up Buddhists. It would be a grave mistake to think that the spiritual treasure that Buddhism points out is the exclusive property of members of the Buddhist club. It is not. Encounters with adhisthana occur wherever people awaken to spiritual reality. These may get recognised or not, but that does not detract from their significance in the lives of those who take refuge in them, or those who benefit from their transformation. There has been an unfortunate tendency for people who are more concerned with power than with spirit to treat lineage as a kind of qualification in which what matters is whether one has the right pedigree, or even the right papers. The adhisthana that is where Amida Buddha is found, however, is universal. True lineages are those made up of teachers who rely upon it. However, as soon as one says a sincere nembutsu one is standing on that ground.

This is a bit like one of the founding issues of Protestant Christianity: the assertion that each believer stands naked in confrontation with God, with no priest or priestly lineage in between. Of course Buddhism does not go so far. It does not reject priests, because the priest, if true, does dwell in the adhisthana too, but the priest is not the only gate. So guru power is a sub-set of lineage power and lineage power is a sub-set of other power. In Pureland we are always concerned with other power. The teacher points it out, supports one through one's encounter with it, is a loving friend and fellow disciple of Amida Nyorai and all other Buddha-Tathagatas. Devotion to the teacher can be just as powerful in Pureland as in any other branch of Buddhism and some, such as Rennyo, did think it essential, but in Pureland the teacher regards himself simply as another disciple of the Tathagata. It is precisely because he does so that he is in adhisthana.

When one is a disciple one looks up to the Buddhas. One's assessment is vertical. When one is a Buddha one's assessment is horizontal. All equal. Reverence (the cure for egotism) rightly abases itself. Love, however, knows no distinctions of rank. Adhisthana is both universal and particular and it requires the asymmetry of vertical and horizontal. Sometimes one is disciple and sometimes one is Buddha. Adhisthana is the ground on which Buddhas stand: emptiness.

All Buddhism is good. Om Ami-dewa Hrih is Namo Amida Bu.

> Even the dull stones
> come alive as he passes
> and turn into bread.
> Though I strive to worship him
> he raises me up instead.

Why do Buddhas Put Out Their Tongues?

Question: In the Smaller Pureland Sutra, also called the Amida Kyo, many Buddhas put out their long broad tongues encompassing many universes and in the Lotus Sutra chapter 21 Shakyamuni does so. Why is this?

Short answer: To demonstrate that they are Buddhas and to display the Dharma.

Longer answer: It was a practice of Indian yoga to cut the membrane under the tongue and extend the tongue by exercises little by little until it could touch the nose. When the tongue is freed in this way, it could also be turned back into the throat and this formed part of a set of yogas that were to do with reducing the body metabolism rate until the yogin could, for instance, survive under water for extended periods. There is a presumption that Shakyamuni during his period of yoga training prior to his enlightenment mastered practices such as these. Exactly what the doctrinal background in ancient Indian religion was I am not sure. The long tongue is, however, one of the traditional marks in Indian lore of a highly developed being. Most of the marks are visible to the casual observer, like the protuberance that you see on the head of a Buddha in statues, or the long ears, but the tongue, of course, is not. A yogin might, therefore extend his long tongue as a way of demonstrating that he was in fact an advanced yogin. Thus extending the tongue came to be a mark of validation when a spiritual being needs, on a special occasion, to demonstrate what he is.

There is also the symbolic aspect that the tongue symbolises the teaching. Extending the whole tongue — more of the tongue than ordinary people are able to do — symbolises that the teaching of a Buddha is completely on display. There is nothing hidden or deceitful about it. The word tongue also means language. The disciples of Jesus spoke in "tongues". Language is communicative code. Only "our people" understand our speech. However, Buddhas, in a certain way, speak a universal language, the language of love, compassion, joy, sympathy and peace. The Dharma encompasses the whole universe. Thus the Buddhas of the ten directions all put out their long broad tongues and teach this Dharma.

> To savour the falling Dharma rain
> old Buddha opened his mighty mouth
> and then sufficiently refreshed
> he put out his tongue
> to scandalise the world.

Isn't Pureland More Like Christianity Than Like Buddhism Itself?

Question: The more I reflect upon it the more I am convinced that Pure Land Buddhism is closer to Christianity than to Buddhism itself. This is shown not only by the emphasis on faith above all else, but also on the idea about how foolish we are. The best testimony that I can think of right now in this regard is Dostoievsky's 'The Idiot', consciously Christian all throughout. But so many other Western artists and writers come back to the same feeling: that of being nothing but a speck of dust compared to the grandiosity of the universe or God. In fact, if we look at things closely it is one of the very basic themes of Western philosophy and arts. I have studied Buddhism quite a bit especially in the last couple of years, and I won't say, of course, that this aspect of "fear and trembling", as Kierkegaard would put it, is absent in Buddhism as a whole, but it is definitely not as present as in the Christian or other monotheistic (semitic) traditions. You might not agree with me at this point, but I think that Buddhism, at least the way it was taught originally by the Buddha, leans a great deal more towards knowledge than to faith or surrender. This is not to say that Pure Land Buddhism is not Buddhism — it is Buddhism in its own right, and sprouted out of certain historic-cultural conditions that made it the way it is. Just as Tibetan Buddhism resembles traditions that were already established in the area or nearby (art-wise and philosophically), so happens with all the rest. Tibetan Buddhism is of course Buddhism, but it is in so many ways so close to Maniqueism, Christian Gnosticism and other non-Buddhist sources that one wonders about labels altogether. It is interesting to me, in this respect, that you use the Buddha as your main reference point all throughout your books, since the tone and the underlying attitude is not, in my view, that Buddhist, but, as I said before, generally Christian.

Short answer: Pureland is Buddhism itself without the Christian-like elements taken out.

Longer answer: Pureland is Buddhism itself. It is true that Pureland is somewhat different from much of the Buddhism that is presented in the West, but there are reasons for Western Buddhism being generally presented the way it is — a way that is rather different from how it is presented in much of Asia. But if we go back to fundamentals for a moment, in most lists of qualities valued by the Buddha, faith comes first. Everything else follows. The term bombu in Japanese that is translated into English as "foolish being" means "being of klesha nature" and klesha is a term used all the time by Shakyamuni. You are right that Shakyamuni puts great emphasis on "knowledge" of a certain sort, but his point is that the vast majority of people (i.e. us) lack that knowledge — thus we are foolish beings. Furthermore there is a linguistic problem. When we hear the word "knowledge" we tend to think about book learning and facts. The "knowledge" that is important in Indian philosophy is not an accumulation of concepts, it is familiarity. If I know you it is because we are familiar with each other. Buddha wants us to know the Dharma in that way.

Western Buddhists do not tend to emphasise faith and familiarity as much as Shakyamuni did and do not generally give devotion the prominence that they have in Asian Buddhism. So, I submit, Pureland is closer to "Buddhism itself" than it is to Western Buddhism and this is, surely, because Western Buddhists are somewhat allergic to anything that reminds them of Christianity so that Western Buddhism is only a selection out of Buddhism itself, a selection that excludes the elements that are Christian-like, hence Buddhism itself is bound to seem more like Christianity than Western Buddhism. To restate this:

Western Buddhism = (Buddhism itself) minus (faith, devotion, klesha-nature, anything else that looks Christian...)

Hence Buddhism itself is closer to Christianity (and most other religions) than Western Buddhism is. It should not surprise us to find that there is a fair bit of common ground between major religions. Having said that, klesha nature and Purelnd teaching have nothing much to do with "fear and trembling". The Judaic God may have been something to fear, but there is no equivalent in Buddhism, certainly not in Pureland. What we fear are not the higher powers, but the world of samsara.

> *"Pureland derives from the very earliest days of Buddhism, from the teachings of Shakyamuni himself."*

Similarly, Pureland is not about surrender in the sense understood by the monotheisms. It is about refuge which is certainly the bedrock basis of "Buddhism itself". I will not take up your points about Tibetan Buddhism — I am sure that most Tibetan Buddhists I know would take issue with you — but it is not my brief. I hope this explains things a bit. Pureland is Buddhism itself, that is, it is faith in ultimate refuge as taught by Shakyamuni and all other Buddhas. Pureland has its own styles of expressing that faith — nembutsu and so on — but style is not the essence. Pureland derives from the very earliest days of Buddhism, from the teachings of Shakyamuni himself and there is actually no legitimate school of Buddhism that does not teach the deluded nature of the vast mass of humanity, no school that teaches fear of Buddha (with or without trembling), and no school that does not teach faith. They may not emphasise these features in the West, but it is so.

> Under every stone I turn
> a Buddha sits in meditation
> or springs forth
> on gilded wings
> to teach the world
> of ancient things.

What is Meant by Saying: Good Ultimately Prevails?

Question: I recently listened to a talk that you gave, as part of the Vow 22 study programme. There was reference to five spiritual laws[*]:

1. The universe is not answerable to my personal will
2. Dependent origination
3. Karma is inexorable
4. Good ultimately prevails
5. Longing springs eternal

Could you say a little more about these, particularly the fourth, "Good ultimately prevails"?

Short answer: Good actions do not necessarily bring immediate result but they always do eventually bear fruit.

Longer answer: These maxims describe the broad framework of Buddhist thinking. Of course, some thinking might implicitly or explicitly challenge them, but they describe the tenor of much Buddhist thought. We start from the existential issue that we

---

[*] Based on the five Niyamas

are in a universe that seems to go on quite independently of us and persists whether we do or not. Indeed, we seem to be a function of it. This realisation is an important first step. It punctures our sense of omnipotence.

Everything in this universe arises in dependence upon causes and conditions, our own mental states not excepted. In this respect, Buddhism is not unlike modern science in its basic philosophy. This, however, is only a background philosophy since Buddhism is essentially a spiritual path. It has more to say than just this. Given that we are in an inexorable universe, how should we live, what can we do? Buddhism suggests there are higher laws — spiritual laws — in addition to the ones that account for the mechanical aspects of the world. These are the laws of karma, of good prevailing and of our inextinguishable spiritual longing.

These three define our spiritual life. We are beings who come into this life not as a blank sheet, but laden with karma. The Pureland understanding of this is that we are foolish beings. Yet, although we have all kinds of delusions and tendencies that bring pain and suffering into the lives of ourselves and others, there still is another way. There still is a path of light where good prevails. This is a second step, if you like. Initially, having recognized this, we think to follow this path by our own effort and so conquer the problem set by the world of Mara. Our despair has as its frame our recognition that we so seldom manage to follow this simple path of love.

The path of goodness — the Eightfold Path — is that upon which good ultimately prevails. It does not always proximately prevail, of course. Sometimes we have to persist through many difficulties. This is because there is always still a residue of old karma which has to be worked through. Old wheels continue to turn, but if one were to persist upon the path of goodness, eventually it prevails. When we fail to do so and then examine ourselves, what we find is some failure of faith. Faith rather than will-power is the vital ingredient. Where there is complete faith one does not really falter. Everything somehow works out. We all long for the good and this longing draws us back toward faith while our experience of short term setbacks in life tend to undermine or reroute our faith. But this undermining only works when there is some chink in our faith in the first place. Pure faith is intrinsically stable. When pure faith is born in us we are very fortunate.

Sometimes pure faith exists within us, but we do not realise that this is the case. The other day I was involved in a discussion with several other people and listening to them talk I suddenly realized that I have complete faith that when we are engaged in this activity of creating a Buddhist community, the eternal Pure Land is present in that activity. I have complete faith in that. Even though I do not necessarily know what the next step is or what we will be doing in this respect next year, I have no doubt at all that in this activity of creating a Buddhist community together the eternal good is present. Not only is it present, it is indestructible. This certainty in no way reduces the fact that I see all of us who are involved in this task — and myself most acutely — as foolish beings. The good that always prevails does not reside in me nor in the next person. It is not a property of persons, it is a property of purposes. This is why Buddhist ethics is so much about intention.

When we sing Tan Butsu Ge* we are reciting the words of Dharmakara Bodhisattva when he was at an early stage of his bodhisattva career. On the one hand, his sincere aspiration is full of naive grandiosity. On the other hand, it completely expresses the eternal good that wells up in him as an unassuageable longing. Oh, if only I could make a perfect Pure Land, he seems to be saying, then everybody would find peace. That would be wonderful, wonderful. And in the activity that springs from such faith, the Pure Land is immediately present in all its fullness. I don't know how to explain it better than that.

> Good is sovereign, good is great,
> yet how we stray away from faith!
> Or rather take our faith elsewhere
> and trust in dross and try to fix
> the world of greed and hate and care
> with cleverness that all goes wrong,
> with discount glue that comes undone.

---

*From the Larger Pureland Sutra, regularly recited in our morning service

Are Some People evil?

Question: I guess most "wrongdoing" comes under the heading of avidya but what would your view be regarding those who behave extremely and with no sense of fellow feeling, as though they are manipulating insentient objects — those who are labelled as sociopathic or psychopathic — as though there is some missing wiring?

Short answer: We all are wrong doers. We do, however, have the ability to sometimes see how acting upon our perverse nature brings undesirable results.

Longer answer: "Evil" is everywhere. It is a potential in everyone. In Buddhism, however, we understand it as avidya — 'not seeing'. We have all done harmful things, but we did them not seeing what we were doing. This is like the words of Jesus on the cross — "Forgive them for they know not what they do". Often we know not what we do and in not knowing we "kill Buddha" as Keizan Zenji says — "No life can be cut off — do not kill Buddha".

Then again, we are all caught up in collective acts of great cruelty. No serial killer has done any worse than our governments have done in our name. We human beings are exceedingly destructive. The Japanese would say we are all akunin. Aku means wrong-doing. Nin means person.

I have worked with people who had been diagnosed as psychopathic, but I have yet to encounter anybody who was really different in kind (rather than just degree) from you or I. As Buddha said, it all depends on conditions. We are all capable of manifesting as hell beings given the appropriate circumstances. Facing this reality is lesson one and we all do well to do revision on it periodically.

Recently there has been a case in the news of a man who killed his girlfriend by stabbing her many times. He was a satanist. Satanists are people who have insight into the akunin nature of the human being, but who then think that if that is what we are like then that should be how we act. Lesson two is that just because something is literally "natural" does not mean that it is a good thing. Many things that are natural leave a very distressing aftermath. In fact, Nature can be exceedingly ruthless.

Naturalness alone, therefore, is not an adequate guide. In our natural state we are not that admirable. We can understand something better. Each spiritual system has its own terminology. In Pureland we call the "something better" Amida in the Pure Land. This is the basic position of the human being: akunin facing Amida. The useful power that we have in ourselves is the power to perceive Amida, but this is not really our own power at all. It is more like the "power" that a mirror has or that the moon has to reflect the light of the sun.

> When his evil heart was opened
> we all had to look away
> the light was so bright.

What Does The Amida Logo Mean?

Question: I noticed on the Amida homepage, what appears to be a logo for Amida Shu? What is the meaning behind the picture?

Short answer: The setting sun behind clouds symbolises Amida's Light imperfectly perceived.

Longer answer: The picture shows the setting sun partially obscured by clouds. This relates to a vision of the sage Shan Tao. The setting sun represents Amida Nyorai far away in the West, symbol of complete enlightenment, object of our longing. The clouds symbolise the obscurations in our nature that prevent us from seeing Nyorai clearly. When we become aware of the clouds we feel very sad, but we also get insight into our nature and this gives access to fellow-feeling for all beings adrift in the ocean of samsara. We thus have the light of Nyorai and the joy it brings as well as the clouds of karma and the sadness, hence the bitter-sweet flavour and the enigmatic nature of Pureland.

In the Contemplation Sutra Queen Vaidehi has a spontaneous opening or vision of the Pure Lands of all the Buddhas and chooses that of Amitabha. Ananda, who is present, is impressed by what has happened and asks how one can get such a vision. The Buddha then describes a series of visualisation meditations by which one can get an approximation of the experience of the appearance of

Sukhavati. This series begins with visualising the sun setting across an expanse of water. The setting sun is a key element in Pureland practice. Temples are sometimes situated especially so that they get a good or auspicious view of the setting sun. The Pureland path is sometimes referred to as a 'westward journey' (Saigyo) or a journey into the sunset. The flavour of Pureland is the feeling that one may get watching a fine sunset — a mixture of awe, melancholy, peacefulness, appreciation of beauty, and vague longing. All of this is indicated by the Amida logo.

> We stood and watched as the sun went down —
> slow motion — a cascade of orange light
> with bands of cloud across the disc
> and peace crept gently over us
> and love in each from each to each.

A Few Questions on The Amida Shu Perspective

Question: Why does the Amida Sangha use the term Pureland rather than Pure Land?

Answer: We read Sukhavati and Jodo, not Sukha Vati or Jo Do, so Pureland is actually closer to the Sanskrit and Japanese. There is no particular basis for thinking that "Pure Land" is somehow "correct". However, that matters little. Language should not be a strait jacket. Language is a convention for communication. There is a usefulness in having separate terms to indicate the style of Buddhism on the one hand and the domain of a Buddha on the other, so the Amida Sangha has adopted the convention of using Pureland for the former and Pure Land for the latter. It works. If others like it they can follow. If they don't, they don't have to.

Question: Why has Amida Shu produced its own version of the Larger Pureland Sutra?

Answer: Well, it's a free country. There is no particular reason why they shouldn't. Actually there are about seven extant versions of the supposedly "original" sutra. The one that has become standard in East Asia and is used by, for instance, Jodoshinshu almost certainly is not the original Indian version. About a third or more of the text originated in China at a later date. Also, much of the original material is, in fact, extremely confused. The main point is that the craving to get a pure orthodox text is a Western obsession that has its roots in

Western religious history and the persecution of heresies. The Buddhists of the past were not bothered about this. What they wanted was a text that would work as a vehicle for conveying the Dharma. Texts are tools, not criteria. The teacher Shinran, for instance, takes huge liberties with the texts that he quotes in his works. This is in order to convey the Dharma. This is why there are so many versions. Teachers of old thought nothing of redrafting a passage if the old version was not working for their disciples. Amida Shu likewise is a group of sincere practitioners who need a text that works, not an academic shibboleth. There is, of course, nothing wrong with people debating the value of the particular rendering, but trying to imply that only some people have the right to produce one is censorship and elitism.

Question: Why does the Amida Shu version of the three core vows differ from the currently established East Asian one?"

Answer: The point in question is the exclusion verse. In the Jodoshinshu version there is a passage at the end of the faith vow that excludes all those who have committed the most grievous sins. This is a doctrinal problem for Jodoshinshu because all of us must have committed them at some time in our many lives so the implication is that the vow is non-functional. This would mean that salvation by faith did not work and the whole Jodoshinshu doctrine would collapse. Various scholars have tried to get round this in various ways. However, not every early version of the sutra has this exclusion phrase situated in this vow. It makes much more sense that this exclusion goes with the vow on salvation by perfecting all virtues. This is logical. The sutra then makes sense and supports the essential

Pureland position (whether Amida Shu, Jodoshin, or Jodo) that perfecting all virtues works in principle but is unattainable in practice so that salvation by faith is the only practical gate. This was the position of Honen and Shinran. This is why the Amida Shu version has it this way.

Question: Surely it is illegitimate for Amida Shu to disagree with Jodoshin-shu, given that Jodoshin-shu is big and Amida Shu is small?

Answer: This, of course is a silly point on several counts. Firstly, size has nothing to do with it. Secondly, in any case, every year Amida Shu gets bigger and Jodoshin-shu gets smaller. But aside from such frivolity, Amida Shu does not actually disagree with Jodoshin-shu doctrinally on anything much so it is an empty debate.

Question: Why does Amida Shu psychologise the Buddhist teaching?

Answer: The Buddhist teaching does not need psychologising, Buddhism is psychology. Buddhism is, as the Dalai Lama has said, a science of mind. It is also various other things — a culture, a philosophy, a religion — but it is about the mind. "All states flow from the mind", says Buddha at the beginning of the Dhammapada. Some people have said to me that Buddhism does not need psychology — meaning Western psychology. In a sense this is true because Buddhism already is a comprehensive psychology in itself. But that does not mean that it can't absorb technical details from other sources — it has been doing so throughout its history. In any case, if you strip Buddhism of its psychology and take all the texts literally then as far as the vast majority of Western people are concerned it would be reduced to superstition. No, psychology is a crucially important gate to the Dharma and the Dharma is psychological as well as being other things too. Again, some people have said that psychology and Dharma are separate in the sense that one could be enlightened and yet still neurotic — I disagree. If you are neurotic you are certainly not enlightened.

Question: What is the Amida Shu perspective on lineage?

Answer: A lineage is a succession of teachers. Most lineages in Buddhism die out. Some new ones form. Each school of Buddhism has its own conventions about lineage. Each has every right to have its own approach, but should not criticise others. The Jodoshin approach is that only blood descendants of the founder should hold high office. If that's what they think, that's fine for them. Those who agree can join, those who disagree can leave. Some schools think that their lineage goes all the way back to Shakyamuni in an unbroken line. This is almost certainly not true, but if it works for them I have no objection so long as they don't start saying that everybody else should think the same. Some say that lineage ensures purity of teaching and conduct. However, some of the worst scandals in the modern history of Buddhism have been committed by long lineage holders.

Half the Zen teachers in the USA belong to lineages that derive from Yasutani Roshi who was, apparently, a Nazi. Some may think that you can be enlightened and still be a Nazi, but I disagree. Knowing who somebody's teachers were is an indicator, but it is not the only indicator and it is certainly not a guarantee.

Sexism in Buddhism

Question: What should we think about sexism in Buddhism?

Short answer: We should lament it, correct it, and not support those forms of Buddhism that practise it.

Longer answer: I was recently talking to a monk of another tradition. He knew that in our ceremonies at Amida the celebrant is often a woman. When the celebrant comes into the room, we all stand to show respect. Actually, it is not really just respect for the person, it is respect for what he or she represents, since the celebrant in a ritual acts on behalf of the whole community. However, this monk would not stand up if the celebrant was a woman. Why not? "It is against our tradition." "But surely that is the wrong thing to do. We should not have sexism in Buddhism." "Well it is just the same in..." he named some other large Buddhist traditions." But, I noticed that you used to do it." "Yes, but I have been thinking about it and I realise I should not do it. It is against the tradition."

This monk clearly thinks that his tradition represents the true Buddhist way. It seems to be true that adherence to his tradition has brought about a change in his behaviour — but it is one for the worse. This is alarming. I sense that his critique actually goes a lot further than just this article of behaviour. He thinks that his tradition is actually the only right one — and I am aware that a great many members of his tradition think the same. This sort of thing deeply saddens me. If the great way of the Buddha is reduced to exclusivism, sexism and condescension, many ordinary, supposedly less enlightened, people will, correctly, very soon realise that it is worthless in that form. What is amazing, however, is that such forms continue to flourish — and are even supported by large numbers of women making a free choice in the matter.

> *"It is... very important that we develop women leaders."*

When one discusses this problem seriously with some other members of such traditions, it is quite common in the West to get a response along the lines of: "Well, yes, it is wrong, and we minimise the effect of the sexist discriminatory rules in our own community, but it would simply be too difficult or complicated to get the rules themselves changed." This means that groups of more enlightened members of such a tradition remain marginalised and disempowered. If you talk to other members of the same tradition, especially those who have spent time in the East, you often get a robust assertion that the male dominated way of doing things is the correct way.

If a tradition is incapable of reforming itself in such an obvious respect, something is deeply amiss. If it is really the case that there is little actual will to change and those in authority in the tradition personally think this kind of discrimination is the true Buddhist way — or just want to keep it that way because they happen to be men in this life — then the situation is even worse. It is, therefore, very important that we develop women leaders in our Buddhist institutions, projects and initiatives so that this antiquated way of thinking is dislodged. In the time of Shakyamuni, there were many women arhats. But where are the records of women arhats after his time? There are not a lot. The tradition fell into the hands of people who had sexist ideas. The Buddha himself did not make rules that were difficult to change — only those who came after did that. Now many Buddhist traditions are burdened by the millstone of statutes that are oppressive that they fear to change. This is not the true spirit of Buddhism and no sincere Buddhist of either gender should conform to it.

> The female devil
> is as fierce as the male.
> Brimstone converted into gold
> is worth the same
> no matter the gender.

Social Engagement

Question: I have been trying to find the real link between Buddhist philosophy and the decision of an individual Buddhist to engage in compassionate action. It seems to me that an objective reading of Buddhist texts would lead one toward a stance of stoicism, since each one of us must endure our karma. How can we help another being who is enduring his or her karma? Providing empathy seems to me an appropriate response, and this is what I so much admired about your approach in Zen Therapy. So often one just wants to be heard and cared about. Fixing the problem (the direction of The New Buddhism) seems like another leap altogether. Thank you so much for your work.

Short answer: Buddha taught compassion for all and established a Sangha that was a social movement, not just an arrangement to support individual practice.

Longer answer: In terms of what has become the mainstream reading of Buddhism in the West you are largely correct to suggest that it implies passivity rather than action. I believe that that reading is unfortunate and is in part a result of the fact that Buddhism in the West began as an object of detached scholarly interest. The resulting objectification misses the depth of religious feeling that made people care enough to carry

Buddhism the length and breadth of Asia. Ashoka sent missionaries far and wide — even to Europe. Why? Buddhism, unlike the other ancient religions of India which certainly do preach resignation, was taken far and wide and adopted in China and in Japan and elsewhere as much for its impact upon society as for benefit to the individual — individuals were not much in focus in those days. Prince Shotoku introduced Buddhism into Japan to bring peace to the nation. The kings of Tibet likewise. The Ambedkarite movement in India is still doing it.

Buddhist liberation is liberation from selfishness. Liberation from selfishness manifests as gratitude and generosity. Gratitude and generosity are not just feelings, they motivate action — action to bring beauty and truth into the world, to relieve suffering and create harmony in communities. When we read the Larger Pureland Sutra, which we at Amida Shu take as the pinnacle of the Buddha's teaching, what we find is a manifesto for a transformed land. Thus, Buddhism is individual and collective. The karma of nations is also to be transcended. The collective life of human beings is the arena within which the Dharma becomes manifest. This is not a matter of making everybody the same — fitting them into a mould — it is the challenge to find a way for diverse people to live in peace and mutual cooperation.

> *"If we do not have the big vision, then empathy can just drag the "helper" down into the same pit as the helpee."*

The religious feeling of this kind of Buddhism is a faith in the Unborn as a transformative force that springs beyond karma. Thus, really Buddhism posits two processes at work. One process is karma, which is a "dead" force. The other process is a life force, an elan vital. Let us call it Buddha Light. Buddha Light leaps beyond karma. For the Dharma life, karma is the spring board. This does not mean that karma ceases to have its effect. It means that something more powerful superimposes, that karma comes to be seen in a new light. Shakyamuni Buddha still reaped the effects of past karma, but because he walked in the Light of Tathagatas he was able to help innumerable beings.

This is really a matter of his faith, but faith is much misunderstood and muddled up with dogmatic belief which is something else. Empathy, as you say, is important, but even more important is it to hold to the intuitive sense of supporting grace or Buddha Light. All Buddhism is about refuge and faith in the Unborn and that is what turns a person around from being concerned about their own gain and salvation to start acting gratuitously which is what the whole idea of the paramitas is about. There is thus nothing new about New Buddhism, it is the same passionate faith that led people in Asia throughout history to lead philanthropic lives and to organise society in ways that took generosity, virtue, energy and so on as ideals in place of self-serving goals.

Empathy should be spacious. If we do not have the big vision, then empathy can just drag the "helper" down into the same pit as the helpee is languishing in. This is why there is a problem of "burn out" in the helping professions. If you treat it just as a technical job, you get pulled down. If you have a bigger vision — big mind, big heart, big faith — then everybody gets lifted up.

Engaged Buddhism should be exactly that, not the importation of "progressive", humanistic or liberal ideas from Western culture into Buddhism. Engaged Buddhism is not really about civil rights, social justice, equality and democracy. These are ideas that have grown out of our theistic Western religious history. Engaged Buddhism is about love, compassion, equanimity, liberation, and harmony. It is less to do with protest and more to do with building an alternative. Engaged Buddhists might cooperate with others in a social justice cause, but they will think about it in a different way. "Justice" can be used as the excuse for almost anything and certainly for punishment. Buddhism accepts that life is not fair — that's karma — but starting from the fact of inequality, it seeks to create a kinder, more cooperative world in which everybody can find a way of being useful and contributing. It is about helping others to help yet more others until there is such a surplus of goodwill that restrictions and coercion melt away.

> Under the samadhi sky
> she fills her apron full
> with lotus leaves on which are writ
> in ink of golden blood
> directions to a finer world
> where there is space for everyone.

Do Social Engagement and Practice Conflict?

Question: From the looks of things, the Amida Trust does a lot of work devoted to thinking about issues of engagement, social issues and Buddhism, and so forth. What are you learning and discovering about how notions of monasticism might be reshaping in the 21st century? Similarly, what have you noticed about new trends in thinking about engaged Buddhism? Is anything apparent to you in terms of what distinct, new energies or ideas Westerners can offer these two areas? As far as you understand my dilemma (do social engagement and practice conflict) do you have any thoughts? What wisdom might your tradition have to offer in terms of thinking about work in the world and the priestly or monastic vocations?

Short answer: The way to become enlightened is to "make offerings to many Buddhas". By doing so we express faith and make ourselves useful. This is beneficial to the world and also satisfies our deepest instinctive needs.

Longer answer: First, the issue of monasticism. Buddhist renunciant practitioners might be called monks, but the original concept was not that of a cloistered person following a rule of stabilitas (staying in one place) which is the definition of monk in most western traditions. The word translated as "monastery", vihara, originally meant "a park". It was the place where wandering travellers stayed for a night or a few days. Buddhist monks were really friars. They were homeless and mobile in basic concept. This is certainly our concept at Amida. Full renunciation implies freedom to go wherever one is needed in the service of other sentient beings. That is what faith and practice mean. The "monastery" should, therefore, be a mother ship for expeditions. People go forth and return. There is then a synergism through sharing. We all learn from one another and grow in faith together.

As for the internal style of monasticism — the liturgical life, the community, the roles and relationships, the day to day work — they should all be shaped to help people learn how to be errant bodhisattvas able to handle responsibility, work diligently, cooperate in harmony with others, remain established in deep faith even in the midst of adversity, trust one another and so on. The monastery (or friary) is a training ground for character, a spiritual power house where people can come and recharge, a mirror for each of us in which we see all the crinkles of our foolish nature. This is where we find out what we are, abandon some of our more glaring pretentions and antisocial quirks, and grow up a bit.

> *"We do not see a conflict between engagement and deepening of practice — they are synonymous."*

Secondly, the question of Western Buddhism and social engagement. Even today Western (and quite a few Eastern) approaches to Buddhism seem to me to be fundamentally at odds with engagement and, in my view, therefore, at odds with what Buddhism is and should be about. I do not see Buddhism as a quest for personal enlightenment that is somehow the property of an individual and I fear that Western Buddhism has taken Buddhist practice and commodified it. Far from understanding non-self ever more deeply and growing in faith, Western Buddhists are all too often just making practice into a personal indulgence and support for introspective rumination. They think that the more disengaged they become the more spiritual they will be and this is a fallacy. An activist friend of mine said: "You see good activists become Buddhists and then you never see them again." In other words, the Western approach is still strongly implicated in quietism. Despite the fact that many people think that Westerners are more world-oriented and extravert than Asian people, broadly speaking, in Asia, Buddhism is a social force as much as a personal one whereas in the West it is not.

In Pureland, I do feel that there is a different outlook — in fact, there is OUT-look rather than only IN-look. For us there is no basic conflict between practice and engagement — they both tend in the same direction and are difficult to distinguish from one another. Practice is faith and faith is tested and strengthened through encounter. Engagement is, therefore, a strong and essential part of our practice. Another strong part is encounter with each other. This yields community, fellow feeling and team spirit, which are all expressions of faith. We have quiet periods as part of the natural rhythm of life, but we would not think that silence matters more than communication, say, or vice versa.

We have developed a system of different forms of commitment and ordination based upon people's availability, which is a function of their degree of renunciation. The more renunciant people are the more engaged they are likely to be. It is the fully renunciant people who are likely to be sent to India or Africa. Others might support them, but they are not free to go. It is important to ask, do I have the faith to do Buddha's work? Do I have the faith to respond to what the universe puts in front of me? Or am I too busy with my own plans for my own salvation to listen to the suffering in the world? What would Buddha have one do?

One might need extra contemplative time to recuperate or digest experience after particularly challenging assignments, but we do not see a conflict between engagement and deepening of practice — they are synonymous. If one really is not free to go forth abroad, then one can go forth locally. Whatever the details, engagement is practice, even if it is engagement with one's housemates or the ants in the garden.

The majority of Western Buddhists seem to be caught in a concept of what Buddhism is that is essentially antithetic to engagement and yet still feel from first principles that engagement must be necessary or right and so finish up in a conflict. I suggest this is a misunderstanding of Buddhism. All Buddha's disciples are bodhisattvas. Bodhisattvas are those who have the faith to do the Buddha's work. Doing the work strengthens that faith. It all points in one direction.

If one thinks that practice is something done when one disengages, one misunderstands practice. If one is seeking something for oneself from the practice, one misunderstands practice. So I would say, "Just have faith and go forth in Buddha's light and it will all take care of itself". A path will unfold. There are people — there are certainly some here — who will be companions for you on the Way and together we (even though we are and remain deluded beings in many ways) become the Buddha body collectively. Buddha lacks for nothing, yet needs something — you. Don't keep him waiting too long.

Socially Engaged Hermit?

Question: I have heard you praise both being socially engaged and also being a hermit. Is there not a contradiction here? One cannot be socially engaged and a hermit at the same time — right?

Short answer: Both are good, but you can't do both at the same time, correct.

Longer answer: By socially engaged, we mean acting in ways that benefit the world. We should also see that the hermit, too, benefits the world. The Chinese have long recognised this. In what are sometimes regarded as "primitive" religions, hermits are often seen as having a vitally important role. The shaman is a kind of hermit. He lives apart from the tribe, but can be consulted. The Desert Fathers were hermits and their lives had a highly formative influence upon early Christianity. Hermits are founts of wisdom.

It is also true that in order to be socially engaged in the most Buddhist manner one needs to be independent. To be a paramita, social engagement must be disinterested. If one's social action is simply in order to get benefit for oneself, it is not the real thing. A bodhisattva like Kuya sees what people need and tries to help. There is nothing in it for him except in a purely incidental way. Now to have that kind of transcendence one needs to have discovered one's fundamental aloneness and gone through it to a place of ease. Being a hermit is one of the best ways of doing so. There is, therefore, a reciprocal relationship between the roles of social action and being a hermit.

> In the forest he conquers fear,
> on the mountain he finds the truth.
> Returning to the market place,
> from a sack that is empty
> he brings forth gold.

Does Faith in The Future Imply Faith in This World?

Question: I'm not sure one can have faith in the future without having faith in a conflicted world (in both senses). There may be a doctrinal point at issue here.

Short answer: Have faith in faith.

Longer answer: Yes, there are all sorts of philosophical and theological issues. A lot hinges on whether you think that everything in the future has to come from the past. It can and has been argued that if the answer is yes, then there is no freedom. Tillich would say that in that case there is nothing truly worthy of the name history — merely development. From a Buddhist point of view, do we think that the doctrine of dependent origination is telling us that everything depends upon conditions and therefore that all of the future depends on the past and there is nothing else to the future than the past unfolded — that the future is simply the implicate order of the past, or do we think that it is telling us that all of that part of the future that depends on the past is already in the province of Mara and that there is something else to be found which is the real (true, eternal) Life of enlightenment etc.? If there is something else — in what is it grounded?

As you say, having faith in a conflicted world has two senses. This conflicted world is the only place in which we can experience our faith at the moment and it is surely because this world is not transparently harmonious and meaningful that faith becomes essential, just to get one through the day, let alone reach any kind of salvation. At the same time, there are deep questions about what it is that we are really placing our faith in. For some people, Amida and the Pure Land are quite closely associated in their mind with this universe. This is basically a Tendai philosophy rather than a Pureland one. Most of the Pureland sages felt that there was quite a lot wrong with the world as it is. Our faith as Amida Buddhists is not in Amida as this world, but in Amida's work upon this and all worlds. Amida's Light penetrates into worlds and we are touched by it and thus become in many unwitting ways, "Bodhisattvas of the earth" and instruments of transformation. There is nothing inevitable about the future. There is no predestination in Buddhism, but there are consequences. So it is not so much a matter of having faith in the future as having faith in faith. We have faith that if we have faith then the future will unfold in a better way than would be the case if we did not.

The Buddhist sense of the bodhisattva is of a being who will act with similar goodwill no matter what world he or she shows up in. If, in my next life, I am reborn in a more conflicted world or a less conflicted world, I hope that I shall be endowed with the same generosity of spirit that I pray the Buddha will give me for my work here in this one. That is what is meant by equanimity — always the same, the same compassion, fellow-feeling, loving kindness, desire to understand — always the same. That is faith. One has such faith here, in this very conflicted world, and having it one has faith that this very world has the capacity to arise in harmony and transcend war, slavery, oppression and conflict.

Is The Buddha Portrayed in New Buddhism Academically Correct?

Question: My own belief is that the Buddha that you portray in your book The New Buddhism is actually the Buddha that you yourself want to become rather than Siddharta Gautama, the historical Buddha. Of course, there is nothing inherently wrong about this. Your ideal is perfectly legitimate and I share it one hundred per cent, but we need to be careful at least from an academic point of view.

Short answer: Academically correct? No! And there is no need for us to treat academe as an ultimate authority.

Longer answer: I am not substantially in disagreement. My book is not academic and I do say in it, I think, that it does not present a balanced academic assessment. It presents my intuitive sense of what Buddha and Buddhism is about. The Amida Sangha is a movement within Buddhism. We have an agenda. If you "agree with it 100%" I'm glad and I am quite happy to let the academics go and be academic. Whether the Buddha was a revolutionary is a matter of interpretation, of course, but it has palpable consequence.

If you go to India today you can witness the Buddhist revolution in the Ambedkarite movement in which millions of untouchables have become Buddhist in an effort to overthrow the graded inequality system of Indian society. They could have become Christians, of course, but they did not see that as the most potent route. Their chosen revolutionary ideal is Buddha and his (their) recent contemporary prophet Dr. Ambedkar. Now this is controversial in Buddhist circles and there are plenty of non-revolutionary Buddhists who will argue for a different interpretation of Buddha just as there are any number of Christians who see Jesus as a pillar of the establishment. Academia has its own agendas and looks at Buddhism and Buddhist texts "from the outside" as it were, whereas we, as Buddhists, look at them as working tools in the enterprise of turning the Dharma Wheel.

> He set the Dharma chakra spinning.
> What a weapon it was!
> Like the wheel that cuts the bread
> he sliced samsara
> and thickly spread
> the golden ghee of hope.

Natural Disasters

Question: How does an Amidist comprehend the incomprehensible suffering and destruction that has resulted from the tsunami disaster this year[*]?

Short answer: As a spur to faith and practice.

Longer answer: We live in a world of troubles where the elements treat us as "straw dogs". We are of no significance to waves and rocks. Everything is impermanent except the Dharma.

> "Even seemingly insignificant beings can be vehicles for universal love."

The uncertainty of our situation — so much emphasised by Shakyamuni — should give us a sense of urgency. Let us think what is most important and get on with it. If we think "I will do it after I have ……. " — fill in your own blank — then we may well be swept away first and never do what matters. A spilt bucket of water might be a tsunami for the ants that live around the kitchen floor. We are no different. There is no point in

---

[*] 2004

building up philosophies predicated upon ourselves as a special case. The universe treats us just like everything else. We are in this existential situation where the wave may come any day. So many people live their lives tossed about, never having done anything that is not trivial. The Pureland perspective helps us to realize that even seemingly insignificant beings can be vehicles for universal love. Even if our life is only a pin prick, it can be the one that lets light into the dark world. The light comes from beyond. It is precisely because we live in a tsunami world that faith is necessary and central to our existence. To live a noble life even as the tsunami is bearing down upon us is what old Shakyamuni asked of us.

> The tsunami is coming,
> be sure of that —
> the grumbling gods will rise.
> How precious is this interlude
> of human life
> before the tide!

What is The Buddhist View of Romantic Love?

Question: Maybe when I've read Zen Therapy I will understand myself a little more. Right now I'm in a wave of emotion they call love, but I would liken it more to an addiction, with painful withdrawal symptoms... I've always felt that I was missing my other half, but despite that I'm still not convinced that it is an answer. I can't say I really understand how procreation, sexuality and love fit within the Buddhist model, at least the engaged Buddhist model, because I can't be intimate with someone without getting wrapped up in the emotion of it: it's the rapture that gives it intensity, but also anguish.

Short answer: Relationships can be a spiritual path, but they are commonly full of delusion.

Longer answer: Sexual love, as you say, has great power to create anguish, rapture and confusion. The Buddha gave it up completely, but that was after having explored it rather thoroughly. If people were more aware of the down side of it, there would be a lot less misery. People would enter into commitments less rashly and, having entered into them would be less easily tempted to break them. It isn't all it's cracked up to be in the commercials. This, however, is principally because people tend to go into relationships in order to get their own narcissistic needs met rather than out of a real care for, or even sufficient knowledge of, the other person. But then, how can one really know another without such an exploration? — "Catch 22".

Romance can seem almost a substitute religion, promising to bring a kind of salvation in which all our deficiencies will be healed as if by magic. The reality is different. When the glitter has worn off, an intimate relationship challenges us to become more mature, or it becomes a spiritual trap in which we collude in co-dependency. The very things that charmed us in the other person become irritants. Power struggles develop.

> *"Trying to do all the things expected of a monk while running a family and holding down a career is just asking for trouble."*

A good relationship can be a real spiritual path since it involves intensity of concern for an other and this can take us out of self in a not merely superficial way. It challenges us to reach a deeper level of honesty. A harmonious couple can bring great benefit not only to themselves, but to everybody they meet. Even a conflicted couple can be learning a lot along the way.

Reflecting this reality, within the Amida Order there is a place for both married and celibate persons. Celibate people can devote themselves wholeheartedly to the path without distraction. Married couples in which both partners are devotees can work as a team and advance together. Married couples in which only one partner is pursuing the spiritual life can present a more difficult situation, but it depends upon the attitudes of those involved. Within the Amida system it is possible for the Buddhist partner to be a lay member or ordain so long as there is real agreement from the other party. The really difficult situations are those where people are committed to a partner who actively opposes their faith. Here it is for the couple to work out themselves what the real meaning and importance of their relationship is and why they are set in such a conflict with one another if they really do care for one another. The Pureland forms of Buddhism, particularly, tend to value lay and family life as wholesome ways to express the Dharma. Much of Buddhism as we have it today is in the forms evolved for renunciant celibate monks and nuns. That is good, but there are few people nowadays who feel capable of such a path. Trying to do all the things expected of a monk while running a family and holding down a career is just asking for trouble. It is too much. Pureland practice offers a more generic form of spirituality, deriving directly from the Buddha, suitable for lay life. Nonetheless, within the Order we do value the more renunciant roles. Really we are presenting a modern version of the kind of structure that Shakyamuni developed with lay and renunciant roles acting in complementary ways.

It is important to recognise that at different stages of life people are best served by different arrangements. We should not judge marriage or relationships solely by how long they last. A long lasting relationship may be stagnant. A short lived one might, for all its brevity, yield some crucial spiritual advance for the people concerned. There are many permutations of conditions and we are continually learning. When we are in love we want it to last forever. A year later we might think differently. Yet, have we learnt? Often people make the same mistake over and over again and seem blind to their own part in it.

In the past, the social institution of marriage was more circumvented by (and supported by) conventions that nowadays have less force in most Western countries. Relationships are consequently more diverse in form and there is a bigger element of "make it up as you go along". This is challenging. Coupled with the fact that people live much longer, this means that we now live in a world of serial relationships to a large degree. This is not all bad, but it can be painful sometimes.

As you say, romantic love is a kind of addiction. One hopes that it will prove to be a benign one and sometimes that is the case. A lot depends upon the goodwill and real care of the people involved. There is a vast difference between real love and mere possessiveness of "need".

> They fell in love
> and then in hate
> and then came solace all too late
> by which the wheel was set in spin
> on which to do it all again.

Phantasy and Transference

Question: I should like to ask you about two things that seem absent from Buddhist meditation as currently practised. One is the transference and counter-transference. I don't mean that these phenomena don't exist in meditation. Far from it! But they seem rarely to be worked through and dissolved or transcended. The other is the realm of phantasy expressed in the transference, in dreams, and in other ways. This can of course involve very primitive emotions and even psychotic rage. To put it concisely: is the "paranoid-schizoid position" a "hindrance" (= a nivarana in Theravada terminology)? I know that these matters feature in various schools of Buddhism (as in the various "Worlds" or mental states of Buddhist iconography), but my own experience of meditation (admittedly mostly vipassana) is that they remain largely abstract rather than immediate and personal and so I wonder whether meditation can effect real and lasting personality change or whether — as such critics as Arthur Janov and even Jack Kornfeld have suggested — it tends to suppress problems rather than getting rid of them. I suspect that you have already considered such questions as these: I'd like to know your views if you'd like to tell me them. Not — I hasten to add — that my experience of psychotherapy has been any better!

Short answer: Buddhist practice involves working through these issues even though this language is not the language Buddhists use.

Longer answer: I agree with you about transference and counter-transference being phenomena that are not well understood in (some) Buddhist circles. They are a problem in relation to meditation, but become a major item when it comes to teacher-disciple relationships where all manner of acting out can occur. Good Buddhist teachers that do not have psychological backgrounds do, I am sure, work through this situation in their own way without verbalising it in psychodynamic language, by being solid in their caring and genuineness and relatively immune to "games", but this can produce a quite rough ride for both parties. I do not think that the kinds of problems you refer to can generally be worked through by meditation alone and meditation may even be contraindicated in some cases where phantasy or paranoid states predominate strongly. It is through (a) the dynamics of the teacher disciple relationship; (b) the dynamics within a Sangha group; and (c) the process of deepening faith; that these dysfunctional dynamics are "worked through". Meditation is not automatically benign. It depends upon the context in which it is employed.

> "The Buddha's words, "This is not me, this is not mine, this is not myself," can be a lifeline."

A person comes to a teacher and becomes a disciple. This almost invariably involves some element of regression and that, in turn, activates infantile and adolescent material. This may be narcissistic, in which case the disciple will idolise the teacher until they can do so no longer, whereupon they are likely to become enraged with the teacher for not fitting in to the projection. A good teacher will sympathise, but remain somewhat rocklike through all this, cherishing the disciple in a kindly manner without getting inflated by the projection. The disciple might manage to work their way through it or might go off in confusion. Even in the latter case, however, some progress will have been made that will ripen later. The inexperienced teacher, however, is likely to be seduced by the idolisation and then infected by the rage and a very troublesome kind of relationship will ensue. One can only pity both parties.

However, the regression may take a neurotic rather than narcissistic form, in which case a rather different kind of seduction comes into play with the disciple trying to induce the teacher into the counter-part to the role with which they have most difficulty. Such role pairings are most likely to be either that of authority or of romance. Again, a good teacher will continue to be there for the disciple without getting hooked.

Of course, teachers are human. One cannot expect there to be no counter-transference. What one hopes for, as a teacher, is that one can see at least part of it and take a relaxed view. The Buddha's words, "This is not me, this is not mine, this is not myself," can be a lifeline at such times.

Looking into the mirrorlike pool
Narcissus, in danger of drowing,
was rescued when he saw the dragon
was only himself frowning.
Passion stirs like an eel -
beware the electric tail!

Can we be Enlightened Yet Still be Overwhelmed by Our Animal Nature?

Question: Dear Dharmavidya, Thank you very much for making the Introduction to Pureland course available — it was always stimulating and often challenging. I valued it very much. At the end of the last unit you asked some questions about the nature of enlightenment. The thought occurred to me that our current understanding of the triune brain might have some bearing on the matter. Simplistically, is it possible to be "enlightened" in the neocortex but then, at another time, be overwhelmed by impulses from the mammalian and reptilian levels? I have recently been practicing Nien Fo in my personal meditation time. Soon after I started, I noticed some ways in which I was relating differently to others. It does seem to be a practice that directly impacts the heart. Who knows, I may yet become a Pureland Buddhist!

Short answer: If we are enlightened to our animal nature we will treat it kindly but firmly.

Longer answer: The two parts to your question are closely related. The Nien Fo practice is designed to help us base our spiritual practice upon acknowledgement that we are "foolish beings of blind passion", or, you could say, that we have a reptilian dimension to our being. Wisdom and enlightenment are then seen more in the frame of achieving compassion for all through knowing our own nature than in the perspective of attainment to an ideal state that the "reptile" is never going to acknowledge. The idea that the wise person is the one who knows just how foolish he is is, of course, not unique to Pureland Buddhism, but it is something that can be lost sight of in the midst of all the wonderful descriptions of transcendent perfection that fill the pages of works of many schools of Buddhism. From the Pureland point of view we are not awakened to our intrinsic perfection so much as to our inner animal. The reptile needs care and attention and some boundaries, but even Buddhas have got one. Acknowledging deeply that we are all in the same boat in this respect is likely to change the way we relate to one another. It, as you say, directly impacts the heart.

> Leviathan
> swiftly from the deep
> swiftly to hide once more.
> Manjushri pats him on the head
> with old affection
> long explored.

Does Buddhism Offer Wholeness and Healing?

Question: Could you simplify — where does Buddhism fit with wholeness? I want to do worthwhile inner and outer work, but I can't say I want enlightenment. Complete healing seems more relevant and Western. My understanding of Jung — the spiritual dimension — is relevant.

Short answer: Though we strive to be whole, we are loved as we are.

Longer answer: In the profound spiritual experience that is referred to as enlightenment, there is an overwhelming sense of rightness about things. You could call that wholeness if you like. This is sometimes symbolically represented by mandala designs, which Jung studied. At the same time, human beings do seem to be characterised by an incurable woundedness too.

The idea of wholeness is a good one if it is taken in an inclusive way. Real wholeness must have a place within it for the unwholesome. Unwholesome impulses arise in the best of us and it does not seem to be possible to arrive at a condition in which this will not recur. So, we are foolish beings of blind passion, but we are capable of glimpsing and even, rarely, seeing clearly, though ephemerally, a glorious and wonderful other way of being that then again fades. This is the nature of the human condition. Our ability to do worthwhile outer work is, in large measure, a function of our ability to see that this is so since from it comes, on the one hand, the capacity for real empathy, and, on the other, the antidote to judgmentalism.

> "Real wholeness must have a place within it for the unwholesome."

Buddhism is a religion. It thus has many dimensions and applications. Healing is certainly one of these. Buddhist holy men, wandering from place to place, must often have functioned as healers, doctors and therapists, applying remedies, teaching methods for healthier living, bringing solace and consolation. One of the famous dialogues of the Buddha is called the Snake Simile Sutta. The simile involved concerns a person wanting to obtain snake venom from a snake. It tells how there is a right and a wrong way to get hold of a snake. Now the only reason for getting snake venom is for making medicine. No doubt, the Buddha's disciples knew and applied such methods. Healing is intrinsically a good thing and there are a variety of Buddhist related healing arts. Tibet was known as the "land of healing" because of the medical skills of Tibetan practitioners.

However, Buddha also taught enlightenment and enlightenment is not simply the result of a progressive healing process. It is rather a change of outlook and feeling that comes about through a radical and abrupt change. The enlightened person is no longer especially concerned about his own healing or recovery. He or she has, rather, become a mirror for the world. If they have a healthy body and mind, that may be an asset, but really it is a condition where that does not matter anymore. The ordinary person has no wish to be thus. He or she is concerned with a more ego-centric agenda, with self-actualisation rather than with liberation.

What is most Western is difficult to disentangle because there are many confusions of terminology here. "Self-actualisation" sometimes means asserting a "self" and sometimes letting it go into a condition of "flow". "Wholeness" sometimes means the wholeness of oneself, sometimes of the cosmos. Western terminology is not consistent. "Complete healing" might mean self-perfection or it might mean enlightenment. A skilful teacher might use Western language, but give it new meaning. Another teacher might use a lot of Buddhist terminology, but really be simply recycling Western ideas in disguise.

As for "wanting enlightenment", it is something one can pray for, but it is not in one's personal power to make it happen. The ego cannot defeat itself. Faith is the starting point, but even that cannot be contrived. Somehow, through some grace, we may arrive at a sense that the self is not the measure of things and that there is a way of being in which what one personally wants is not the fundamental criteria of life. Western therapy is concerned, by and large, with showing the individual how to get his "needs" met. Enlightenment is about letting them go. The former may bring one to a certain wholeness of self, but the latter to a wholeness that transcends it.

Similarly wanting "wholeness" or "complete healing" is asking the impossible. You might have a satori in which you know that you are identified with the whole cosmos, but, as Jack Kornfield so rightly says, "After the ecstasy, the laundry." One has to come back to earth. In Zen, one inflates the ego until it bursts. In Pureland one deflates it. Two paths, one purpose.

> I want to be whole, the young man said.
> The old man smiled and poured the tea.
> How can I do it?
> How can you not?
> But I want to be special!
> Then whole you are not.

Anxiety

Question: As a background to my question, I would like to explain that since I was very young (my parents say six) I have had periodic episodes of anxiety and panic due to thoughts about the uncertainty of death, not understanding who we are and why we are here, leading to an overall sense of meaningless and hopelessness. This has reoccurred several times over the years. I am now 43. I discovered eastern religions, starting in high school, through books, felt a real connection to the concepts, but never engaged in practice. In the past few years my interest resurged and I bought a number of new books, including Zen Therapy, which probably impressed me the most.

I have read it a couple of times. This got me interested in some form of practice. I didn't know any groups here so I have been meditating on my own, but don't feel much is happening. This year I have suffered two really extreme periods of anxiety and panic. I am currently having another serious episode of anxiety and panic. I cry a lot. I really need help. I read on the questions part of your website the following advice: "I would not recommend meditation to anyone with major psychiatric illness as what people in that condition generally require is not more introspection but more reality contact. I would be wary of offering meditations that involve attention concentrated upon bodily processes, such as the breath, the heartbeat, or other body functions, to people prone to anxiety states or currently experiencing major grief since this may well make them worse rather than better." I don't know whether I would say I have a major psychiatric illness, but I am definitely prone to anxiety states. My question is what course of action is recommended for someone like myself?

Short answer: Reconnect with the natural world in a spirit of awe.

Longer answer: I sympathise. Panic is no joke. Our approach to Buddhism here in the Amida Sangha is based on shinjin. Shinjin is commonly translated as "faith". At a simplistic level we could say "trusting the process of life" or "naturalness". Obviously I do not know a lot about you so whatever advice I give might need some fine tuning. As a broad response to your problem I would say "Go outdoors, look at plants, rocks, the sea, rivers. Don't think over much, just look." We do a practice that is called sunset meditation — we stand and watch the sun set and chant "Om Amitabha Hum" over and over slowly as we watch it go down until the last bit of red light disappears. Or you can look at the moon and chant "Namo Quan Shi Yin Bo Sat". Or you can just look. Don't do this trying to control the anxiety. Do it paying attention to the object — the moon, the sun, the earth, the wind.

Some anguish is natural and appropriate. Life is bitter sweet, comforting and lonely all at the same time. In Pureland practice we channel these feelings into our practice — not to overcome them, but to celebrate the fact that they are what life is all about. We are not trying to be perfect in any way — we are just foolish beings standing in a wonderful light.

Do write more if you wish, but not until you have spent some time with the natural elements. The first meditation that the Buddha gave to many of his disciples was the meditation on the earth element. He would have them spend time meditating on rocks, clay; the solidness of things. Go for walks and feel the earth beneath your feet. Start there.

Addiction

Question: Is it fair to regard Buddhist psychology as primarily a psychology of addiction?

Short answer: In the sense that Buddhism treats all mental pathology as a form of compulsive attachment, yes.

Longer answer: If you study Buddhism you very soon run into the Buddhist ideas about attachment. What is called attachment in Buddhism could as well be called compulsiveness or addiction.

We are all addicted. We are addicted to the strategies that we use in order to avoid aspects of life. Not everybody is frightened of the same things and each person has their strategies of avoidance, but there are general principles that apply and the Dharma is full of advice on this matter. It is perhaps worth noting in passing that what the Freudians call "defense mechanisms" can be more strictly translated as "ways of warding off". In Buddhism this warding off is called avidya, a word which implies intentionally not seeing. The intention, however, may be unconscious.

How does one break an addiction? Generally by clearly seeing the disadvantage. The Buddha does not say that there is no benefit in such attachments nor does he refer to them as sins. The reason for not doing them is simply that the outcome is pain and suffering for oneself and others. Why do we not stop? Because we do not see clearly. Why do we not see clearly? Because we don't want to. This, in simplistic terms, is the Buddhist diagnosis. It seems simple and it is, but our failure to break through these barriers entails enormous self-inflicted pain and trouble for one another.

What are we addicted to? Drugs, alcohol, sex, entertainment, relationships, consumer durables, food, status, power, reputation, pride, and all the other things that we believe we "cannot do without", in other words: all the things that we think of as "needs".

How is it that an intellectual understanding of the disadvantages does not dislodge such compulsive habits? Because we do not have sufficient faith. We believe that these things are our lifelines, and when they are threatened we start to panic. Craving sets in and we soon find ourselves going round the same old cycle again. Along the way all manner of secondary formations occur — self-pity, conceit, self-indulgence, self-assertion — a great variety of strategies for maintaining our sense of control.

How do we get beyond that? The combination of seeing the disadvantage in one course and having faith in another can make us change direction. For this to be more than merely intellectual it generally requires a collision with some factors in tangible reality, both those that inspire faith on the one hand and those that make clear the disadvantage on the other. Thus, Shakyamuni had two great moments of turn around. The first was when he saw the four sights. His encounter with sickness, old age and death showed the disadvantage and the fourth sight, that of the serene holy man, inspired faith. This was enough to turn him from a life of indulgence to one of spiritual seeking. However, this was not sufficient. He took it to extremes and his second great turn around came when he saw the disadvantage of his asceticism through having reached rock bottom at the same time as he was innocently and spontaneously cared for by Sujata whose actions inspired his faith. Then he experienced a great awakening.

The example of Shakyamuni shows us just how bad it sometimes has to get before we are willing to learn new ways. It also tells us that there may be stages. Giving up one folly may move us on, but sometimes only onto another. Some people get off one drug onto another or off one compulsion into something else. This may still be progress. Some are more benign than others. Better to be addicted to chocolate than heroin.

What is it like to be genuinely free from an addiction? Empty. Buddhism talks a lot about emptiness. The ordinary person fears it, which is another way of looking at why we cling and crave. However, the full experience of emptiness is bliss. Ecstasy. This is real liberation. There is nothing better and this is what the Buddhas all wish for us.

Although they wish it for us and give us the Dharma that can inspire us toward it, they also know that we are the kind of blind foolish beings who, most of the time, are only going to turn a blind eye. This is why Shakyamuni was at first reluctant to teach. It took divine intervention to get him going.

So the Buddhas have vast compassion for us in our present state. They do everything they can to create conditions that may help us to awaken. If we can't do it in this life then they may take us to a better place in the next one where the conditions are better. One might slightly sardonically say that, for most people, the Pure Land will be a great clinic where they can get help.

So, yes, Buddhism is a psychology of addiction, not in the sense that it is limited to what we medically classify as major addictions, but in the sense that Buddhism sees how we are everywhere blinded by our compulsive attachments. The Dharma offers a wide range of "methods" to help us, but really there are no techniques that can be guaranteed efficacious. What is required is a cleaner encounter with reality held within a framework of inspired faith. The word Dharma implies that kind of holding. The Dharma holds us while reality teaches us.

All Buddhist "training" can be seen in this perspective. The teacher works through the shaping of conditions and the inspiration of the teachings and the encounter with reality does the rest. Inevitably, however, being all addictive personalities, we are bound to take whatever "practice" we may be given and turn it into another addiction. It may be a less pernicious one, but it is not liberation. There remains a leap beyond, a fall without parachute, and that takes faith.

Some Questions on Zen Therapy

Question: What is the view of Human Nature in Zen Therapy?

Answer: The core of human nature is love. Our love is never totally unconditional, but we can intuit unconditional love. Sensing it, we can realise that we must be objects of it. Although we cannot do it, it enfolds us. Actual love, in a conditioned world, inevitably involves choices, conflicts, frustrations and disappointments as well as joys, satisfactions, creativity and growth. How we cope with and respond to these various challenges and graces makes us the characters that we are. The elements in this mix that we have difficulty resolving crystalize as our personal koan which is our individual manifestation of the universal existential questions about mortality, life, existence and meaning. Thus we love, imperfectly, and meet with setbacks, frustrations and disappointment and we struggle through. It requires faith and courage. Insofar as we have these we become free, rising above the adversity. However, we also learn our limitations and come to appreciate our ordinariness, which then provides the basis for fellow-feeling and wise compassion.

Question: What are the therapeutic techniques and procedures used in Zen Therapy?

Answer: Zen therapy is an approach not a technique. It can make use of almost any therapeutic method — conversation, psychodrama, art therapy, outdoor pursuits, dance therapy, whatever. However, those methods it uses it will tailor to the principles of Buddhist psychology. These are grounded in how we relate to (i.e. esteem) the world around us, using and misusing it, serving and being served by it. Thus Zen Therapy is likely to employ the above techniques in an "object related" manner, expanding the client's comprehension of the world, getting perspective upon his place within it, and developing gratitude and appreciation.

Question: How has your thinking changed about therapy since writing Zen Therapy?

Answer: The Zen Therapy book was written while I was still considerably under the influence of Thich Nhat Hanh. Most of the theory in the book I will still stand by. There are, however, some specific areas where my interpretation has changed. First there is the reinterpretation of the Four Noble Truths as set out in The Feeling Buddha. Second there is a different take on dependent arising as set out in The New Buddhism. I do not think that it is useful to think in terms of "everything being part of everything else" or "everything depending on everything else" anymore because I realised that if you follow such ideas through consistently they undermine ethics. Ethics has to involve choices in which we accept some things and reject others. This also makes me sceptical of many of the common interpretations of "nonduality" and "interbeing" — so many actual relationships are one way: I need the sun but the sun does not need me. I have come to think, therefore, that while interdependence sounds good, the real challenge is to accept our dependency. This also chimes with a growing appreciation of the Pureland perspective on human nature as vulnerable and fallible. So I would only use concepts like Buddha Nature now in a very restricted manner as they too easily play into a human weakness for grandiosity.

Question: Can you say more about what you mean by Buddha Nature and how it reconciles with Carl Rogers' view that "if one is able to get to the core of an individual, one finds a trustworthy, positive center"? (Rogers, 1987)

Answer: Buddha's nature is no nature. A person is as shunya as anything else which means that one can be many things. Some say Buddha nature is the potential to be a Buddha, but that is like saying every plot has palace nature — you still have to build the palace and many people are far from having got it together to build a palace and are busy building casinos, abattoirs or shanties instead.

Many Western people have conflated Buddha nature with the Rogerian idea of an actualised self and/or with the popular spiritual idea of "that of God in everyman" and this expresses the inevitable colonisation of Buddhism by Western popular ideas. Inasmuch as it means "Have a positive regard for others" I have no quarrel with it, except insofar as it confuses the real Buddhist idea. A Buddha is not attached to being reliable or non-reliable, good or bad, trustworthy or non-trustworthy. It is because they are not attached and are able to adapt that, in the ultimate analysis, they really are trustworthy, but this does not mean that they conform to any conventional idea of what that looks like. A Buddha is willing to be whatever the situation requires. Buddhism basically does not have the idea of a "core" in the person. Many people want to introduce this idea and it has been a perennial struggle in Buddhism, at least since Nagarjuna, to resist and refute this notion. It is well meant, but the Buddhist truth goes beyond it.

To me the Rogerian statement comes out like this: when he says "if one is able to get to the core of an individual" he is referring to being genuinely empathic and warm toward that person. If you are genuinely empathic and warm toward a person you will sooner or later encounter the best aspect of that person and you will provide the conditions that maximise their chance of growing in a constructive manner. Buddhism agrees that treating people well is to be recommended and that good things result, but it does not conceptualise this as being due to the existence of a "core", it conceptualises it in terms of likely outcomes from providing conducive conditions.

Question: "Modernists believe in objective reality that can be observed and systematically known through the scientific method. They further believe reality exists independent of any attempt to observe it" (Corey 2009) "Postmodernists, in contrast, believe that realities do not exist independent of observational processes. Social constructionism is a therapeutic perspective within a postmodern worldview: it stresses the client's reality without disputing whether it is accurate or rational" (ibid). Can you comment on these two statements and how they relate to the phenomenological approach of Zen therapy?

Answer: I believe in an objective reality and that Buddhism is about bringing a special kind of objectivity to areas that are often considered subjective. At the same time our capacity is limited. Thus, the Buddhist position is a middle way between modern and post-modern as you have defined them.

Measuring reality does involve interfering with it. In some domains, such as sub-atomic physics, the necessary interference substantially changes the entity being measured and this puts a limit on what one can know. However, what we measure is not the reality itself, it is an abstraction related to the reality. You cannot measure tableness, you can only measure heights or lengths or weights of tables. Heights, weights etc. do not exist. Tables exist. Science concerns itself with the relationships between abstractions, many of which have great concrete usefulness. Science has been successful in demonstrating regularities between these abstractions that are useful approximations to what goes on in the real world.

The scientific method is not, however, some kind of ultimate truth, it is simply a useful method. There has been an unfortunate tendency, well described by philosopher Mary Midgley, to treat science as a kind of neo-religion and scientific method as a kind of religious dogma. This undermines good science as well as leading people astray. Scientific method does some things very well, but cannot, for instance, tell us what we should do. If we know what we want to do then science can often help us to do it. This is like art. An artist may be assisted by science that tells us about how pigments work, but the artist has to do the painting. Therapy is an art. It can be assisted by science, but it is not a scientific procedure. Science yields knowledge of a certain kind, but you could have a vast amount of such knowledge about a client and the client still not be healed, or you might heal them with very little knowledge, just as the painter might produce a very effective minimalist design.

However, whether what the client is saying and doing chimes with reality does matter. Acting unrealistically leads to disasters. Therapy always challenges the client's frame of reference. An empathic reflection, for instance, implicitly calls what is reflected into question. Why does one look into a mirror if not to consider the possibility of altering something? If you don't want to have the possibility of reconsidering your life, don't look into the mirror that the therapist or spiritual guide holds up.

Nonetheless, as therapist, I do not actually always need to know whether what the client says is accurate or rational. If I show him what he is saying he can decide for himself. If he decides well, his life will go better. If he decides badly, it will probably go worse. Well and badly do, here, however, refer to congruence with an objective reality. So the Zen Therapy position is neither modernist nor post-modernist. There is a reality but there are limits to our ability to know it. Whether our lives conform to it affects well-being even though our knowledge of it cannot be total. Life cannot, therefore, be perfected in the sense of becoming totally harmonised with reality. However, we can accept and have faith that, if we are of a generous spirit and a happy disposition, good will come of it one way or another.

A healthy life requires a perspective that encompasses human limitation and the confrontation with reality that is not answerable to one's personal will, as well as the faith and courage to live one's best within such an existential circumstance. In the course of it one will have successes and setbacks and be endlessly learning. It is a challenge not to close down, but to keep facing reality however much dukkha shows up. The task of therapy is, on the one hand, to make that confrontation more vivid and, on the other, to support the faith and courage necessary to optimise the opportunity that it provides.

Buddhism and Christianity

Question: A coincidence between Pure Land Buddhism and Christianity is the way the practice of nembutsu goes, which, as far as I know, is extremely close to that of praying the Rosary. Other common features are Heaven on Earth/Pure Land, but particularly the fact that both are religions for the masses and the poor. Extraordinary coincidences.

Short answer: 1. Buddhism influenced Christianity. 2. Some truths are universal.

Longer answer: Yes — and probably more than coincidences, but in which direction lies the influence? Buddhism is older than Christianity. Where did the Christian ideas come from? not just from Judaism. It is possible to see Christianity as an adaptation of Pureland Buddhism to a theistic ambiance. In all probability religions have been influencing each other back and forth throughout human history. Religions are human artefacts. They reach for something beyond human contrivance, but they are made by people and the process of borrowing goes on all the time in all directions.

Regarding the practices and teachings you single out (1) the mala or rosary has always been used by Buddhists since long before Christianity was invented. A closer analogue to nembutsu in Christianity, however, is the Jesus prayer. It seems much more likely that the Eastern Orthodox Christians got the idea from Buddhism than the other way around. The nembutsu could be translated as "I, a foolish being, call out to the all accepting Buddha" and the Jesus Prayer as "Lord have mercy upon me, a sinner." There is a close parallel. (2) Heaven and the Pure Land are well established in the earliest Buddhist texts which again antedate Christianity by a long time. Buddha, in the Pali canon, says that "those who have faith in me shall go to the Pure Abodes". Jesus says much the same five hundred years later. (3) Mass religion: Buddhism must have been a mass movement from an early stage. Pureland in the Japanese form particularly became a mass religion as a result of the preaching of Honen (1133-1212) but it is very unlikely that this had anything to do with connections with the West, though some people have seen remarkable parallels between medieval iconography in Japan and Europe so we cannot rule out influence altogether. This was, however, before Marco Polo opened up trade between Europe and East Asia. More likely there is here a parallel development. The world was somehow ripe for it at that time.

We should not be worried that some aspects of two great religions are similar. It is confirmatory. It happens that many Western converts to Buddhism are in flight from Christianity and so are somewhat allergic to anything that seems similar between the two religions, but that is a function of transient historical circumstances, not a reliable guide to truth.

Question: Do you have a theory about Jesus from a Buddhist perspective? Was he just a good man, a prophet or what?

Short answer: There are many Buddhas.

Longer answer: Yes, I have a private hunch. I'd put it like this. In the career of an enlightened teacher one observes three phases which we may call preparation, renunciation and ministry. In the case of Shakyamuni Buddha the phase of preparation runs from his birth until he left home and the phase of renunciation runs from then until his enlightenment. His ministry then occupied the remaining forty plus years of his life.

Now my hypothesis about Jesus is rather unconventional. I think that his preparation ran from birth until the forty day retreat in the wilderness. The period that most authorities call his ministry I would call his renunciation period. I think that this was the period when he was still finding out who he was. This period ended with the crucifixion. I find the easiest way to make sense of the events around and immediately after Easter is to assume that he did not die on the cross but was rescued — probably through the influence of Joseph of Aramathea who arranged a tomb for him — something that was generally not allowed for victims of crucifixion. Bodies were usually left on the cross to rot. Jesus was, however, taken down after a mere three days and the next day he was talking to people, so I make the naturalistic conclusion that he was taken down before he was dead and he revived in the "tomb". This idea is not original — see *Jesus Lived In India* by Holger Kersten. If Jesus did not die, he would not have been able to stay around in Roman territory for long, so after making himself known to a few intimates, he went East. Paul subsequently encountered him on the road to Damascus — I take this to have probably been a real encounter, not a mere vision. So, on this theory, Jesus' real ministry as a Buddha took place after the crucifixion, but during that period he would have been a mystery figure to the people in the Roman domains to whom his spokesperson, Paul, delivered the message. There are a number of pieces of evidence that Jesus eventually lived and died in Kashmir.

The earliest New Testament accounts of Jesus are those of Paul, but he says almost nothing about Jesus before the crucifixion. For that earlier Jesus we have to wait for the later writers who produced the gospels. I also suspect that the Three Wise Men were Buddhists — after all nobody else at that time, as far as we know, went about following a star in an attempt to find a incarnated tulku. If this is correct then there would have been Buddhists taking an interest in his early development and contributing to his education which could help to account for the fact that when his parents took him to Jerusalem as a boy he was already a learned prodigy. So my hunch is that Jesus received at least some Buddhist education and, as he grew up had to make sense of this in a Jewish context. This hypothesis helps to explain the interesting mix of Buddhist and Jewish ideas that run through his gospel teachings and the struggles that he appears to have had over whether he himself was a universal wisdom teacher or a specifically Jewish messiah. My hunch is that these struggles and confusions were resolved for him through the experience of the cross. The post-Easter Jesus is a universal teacher and that is why Paul is able to spread the message to the gentiles even though the pre-Easter Jesus had not done so to any significant extent. It also explains why leadership of the Jesus movement did not pass to Jesus' brother and the other followers in Jerusalem. Well, it is only a hunch, but, I suggest, it explains most of the data at least as well as any other hunch that is around in Jesus studies at the moment.

I am willing, therefore, to take it that Jesus was an important Buddhist guru, both before and, especially, after the crucifixion.

> Reborn in the West
> under a star
> he brought peace to the people
> on the path of meekness:
> Blessed are the bombu
> for they shall go to the Pure Land

Question: I was wondering whether you've read much of Don Cupitt's work or had any connections with the 'Sea of Faith' movement? He gave a talk last year[*] called *An Apologia for My Thinking* — an overview of his thinking. I've been reading his Emptiness & Brightness book and it struck me that some of his views about what faith, religion and indeed meaning to life may appeal to you. Certainly, I'd love to hear a Pureland critique of it!

Short answer: Similar concerns, different conclusions.

---

[*] 2002

Longer answer: Thank you. Don Cupitt's work is not something I have looked into before and I have not read Emptiness and Brightness, but I have now read the talk you refer to and I certainly appreciate the philosophical dilemmas that he seems to have been struggling with. It occurs to me that in some ways he has been moving through similar seas to myself, though perhaps travelling in the opposite direction, as I, having considered the same areas of deconstruction and encountered the same nihilistic consequences, have gradually become more tolerant of metaphysics (by which I mean something close to what Iris Murdoch called "the sovereignty of good") and, in particular, have at last come to see the value in "maintaining an unbridgeable gulf between Holy God and the sinful human being", though, as Buddhists, we do not talk about God, but about the ideal Buddha, Amida.

This gulf is not, in Buddhism, at least, "for the sake of social control", but, rather, serves at once, on the one hand, to ground our spiritual life in a personhood and an existential world that never are ideal, whilst, on the other hand, never losing sight of that ideal by which alone our lives can be lifted and inspired. Collapsing one of these poles into the other one seems to me to be spiritually reckless, though I appreciate that many Buddhists would disagree with me. My position in this respect is characteristically Pureland.

I do not see the spiritual life as a journey from the mundane to the divine, the ordinary to the ideal. Rather it is a journey in which both are eternally present as the landmarks by which one discerns a Middle Way. The Middle Way takes into account Amida's illimitable light and my own incorrigible darkness. As a result, I feel accepted just as I am, not as I might become only after scaling whatever spiritual heights there might be, but precisely as I am now, darkness and all. It is precisely this world just as it is that is the place where the spiritual life takes place, and it is here that I discern the "unbridgeable gulf". This does not instil a feeling of alienation, so much as of realism, in the ordinary sense of the word. Anything else smacks of hubris.

Question: [Extract from a longer letter setting out some of Cupitt's views] "Traditionally religions have presented the idea that there is something fundamentally wrong with the human condition (and the world) and so have offered solutions to attain 'salvation' and enter the better state to come (E.g. heaven, Nirvana etc.)"

Answer: I feel I want to say, well, there is, isn't there? How about war, torture, slavery, or, closer to home, everyday nastiness? I suppose I am less sanguine than Cupitt about humans. Saying something is (post-/) modern and human does not recommend it to me. Also, I think his criticisms of the traditional way are a bit overly stereotypic. Is he not setting up a straw man? For instance, in the Western tradition, it was Gnosticism that really polarised heaven and earth and that was declared a heresy for precisely that reason by the orthodox traditions. There is a middle way that recognises human nastiness and offers a better state and that is the Buddhist way, but I think it has also been the way of many traditional Christians too. The idea that "earth is already heaven" is valuable in some contexts, but it is not adequate as a complete dogma because it needs to be balanced by the fact that "earth is already hell" too. Pureland accepts that there is much that is wrong with us, but asserts that, nonetheless, if we give birth to faith, we can become acceptable to Amida, even if we have been cruel, greedy and proud.

This is because faith will work a transformation within us. It will do so because it will open us up to an influence that, because it is not from within, is not corrupted by our past negative karmic formations. Unless we set up something that is good and sublime outside of self, this will not happen and religion will simply become a game of self-congratulation in which we preen our soul, or Buddha nature, or whatever, but never escape from the loop of solipsism.

Awareness of our failings is more important than pride in our virtues. Even in Pali Buddhism, Shakyamuni says that he would rather have a sinner who realised his fault than a complacent saint who, through ignorance, was bound to decline. The idea that "Earth is already heaven" is a bit like "everybody is already inherently enlightened". It is not and they are not. It and they are beautiful and sublime in many ways, but also many other things and dukkha is everywhere.

Question: [second extract] "Traditional metaphysical religion was fixed, unchangeable, firm. It was rock, where contemporary faith must ride the wave, the swell, embracing perpetual motion. But why speak of "faith" at all? Not because we see any merit in "having faith" in unprovable religious dogmas and doctrines. We do not set up "faith" against reason, as metaphysical religion tended to do, nor do we use it as a synonym for blind belief. Faith for us is the trust that it is possible to give value and meaning to life: we can't prove it, but we choose to live by that faith."

Answer: Very interesting. On the other hand, there is certainly some value in religion being a rock. One could say that that is what it is for. The Dharma too is presented as the eternal truth that holds us in the midst of impermanence. There does seem to be some contradiction in saying that there is no merit in "unprovable" things and then setting up in their place something that one admits cannot be proved. In doing so, is one not readmitting what one sought to exclude, which is a faith, call it blind if you like, in value and goodness, that goes beyond the value and goodness that we actually see enacted by the average deluded human being? I think one is right to readmit it and would be better not to exclude it in the first place. We have a sense of virtue that lies beyond us. Goodness is something sovereign that we call to from afar. There is actually very little that is provable in this life and insisting that the other fellow (traditional or not) conform to a higher standard of validity than one intends to adhere to oneself can easily lead us astray.

So, on that basis, surely, metaphysics is only a problem when people make undue claims for it - but then, that is true of anything. To reject something because some people make such claims would lead to the rejection of all worthwhile things, for they are commonly, and understandably, over-sold. A metaphysic should have descriptive, predictive, and normative value. Of course it is man-made — it is a human discipline — just as physics is. However, it tries to describe something that is not man-made — the moral order of the universe. As we say in Buddhism, the law of karma is not answerable to my personal will. Then again, as between mysticism and metaphysics, mysticism does not win every time. For instance, saying that X is the same as not-X is of limited utility and has been seriously over-worked in Western Buddhist circles. Similarly, dismantling all structure relating to our appreciation of the moral realm has serious pitfalls. Of course, no particular metaphysic is the ultimate and unsurpassable — any more than any particular physics is. In physics, Einstein is supposedly better than Newton, but his theory is neither ultimate nor self-evident, and the older system does work better for most everyday purposes. Sometimes this is true in metaphysics too.

I must thank you for your efforts. Debate on these things is very clarifying. I do not think we have reached the last word — that is the nature of the subject, but we have turned up some interesting threads.

Buddha and God

Question: What does Pureland Buddhism say about God, if anything? Are there just Buddhas who are enlightened but no need/place for God? Are they the same thing?

Short answer: Nothing about God with a capital G. Some gods might be Buddhas.

Longer answer: The idea of God that exists in the monotheistic (Abrahamic) religions does not really figure in Eastern thought. There is more a sense of the existence of any number of celestial or supernatural beings, who sometimes have special or extraordinary powers, but they are, as it were, all within the system of samsara, not external judges or creators of it — they are in the same boat as the rest of us. This is the general eastern background. Pureland does not particularly add to nor demolish this general background idea.

Buddhas are enlightened beings. Generally speaking they are human, but they could be gods if that is what it took to help others. Of course, Buddhism also has the idea of rebirth which involves passing from one realm to another, so we might also be gods at various stages in our wanderings through samsara. Perhaps we might think of gods of this kind as a bit more like angels.

When, in interfaith discussions, I have been asked, "Is Buddha a god?" I generally have said that it does not matter whether Buddha is a god or not, but it does matter if your God is a Buddha. If the one you worship is wise, compassionate, patient, accepting, inclusive, gentle and so on, then that one is probably a Buddha and you will benefit greatly, but if the one you worship is punitive, narrow, cruel, intolerant, dogmatic etc., then I am fairly sure that they are not a Buddha, so watch out.

Of course, some characteristics of Buddhas do have something in common with the idea of an all loving god — God with the judgement taken out, as you might say. So some people's sense of God is very close to that of Buddha — an always available, benign, enlightened being who blesses us and invites us to a better life.

The general Buddhist sense is of great multiplicity including many Buddhas, each with particular characteristics, existing in many worlds and times, each offerings particular spiritual pathways, all ultimately in accord with each other but manifesting in ways that help different beings. There is no direct equivalence between the oriental and the middle eastern religions, but if you were to think of a universe in which there is no creator god but many angels you would be somewhere near to the eastern sense of it.

Suicide

Question: This may seem a bizarre question but it's one I that I would like a Buddhist view on. Is suicide a sin? In Christianity to commit suicide is a total sin, it is considered evil and completely against all it teaches but in ancient Japanese culture it was one way of proving total loyalty to one's sovereign Lord. Does someone diagnosed with incurable cancer have the right to end their life on their own terms? Does this create karmic ripples? I know this is a weird question, but as someone who has had a heart attack and a stroke and has been told I face early onset dementia do I have the right to choose when I leave this world?

Short answer: Not an absolute matter in Buddhism — it all depends upon motive and intention.

Longer answer: In Buddhism one has neither "rights" nor "sins", only consequences. One certainly has karma and if an act is intentionally committed in a self-serving manner it will create karmic seeds. Generally speaking, Buddhism cherishes all life and is opposed to suicide. There are instances in the sutras where the Buddha says that there was no fault in a particular suicide because the motive had been purely altruistic. This altruism could be that of saving others from being burdened by the care of one's person when one's medical condition was completely hopeless, but this does not refer to a situation where it is merely the case that, on the balance of probabilities, one is going to get worse and not recover. When a person does commit suicide, the "correct" Buddhist attitude toward them — except in these very rare completely altruistic cases — is compassion (not disapproval) both for what they did suffer and for the karma they have created. The idea of proving loyalty by ritual suicide is not Buddhist, it is a samurai custom deriving, I imagine, from Shintoism (if it has religious roots at all). When we say things like "the right to end their life on their terms" — this is an idea and a form of thinking very much grounded in the Western individualistic paradigm and is not really in the Buddhist mode.

We can take responsibility to use whatever life we have in a noble way for the benefit of all. This is true whatever the extent or limitation of our faculties may be. It is, of course, no easy matter, and we often get it wrong, but the principle is clear enough, I think. It is, perhaps, better to think of life as something entrusted to us than as something that we have power over. We do not know what the future holds and we do not know what influence our mode of conducting life will have, but we can be broadly confident that living in a dignified manner is itself supportive to many beings, including those we are unaware of. In general, suicide tends to undermine the faith of others and cause them dismay and fear.

Currently, there is a certain amount of debate about euthanasia, which has gradually become more popular in Europe over recent years. Again, it is the motive and intention that is crucial and the effect upon others. This is a difficult matter because one does not know the extent of that effect. Different people are affected in different ways. One cannot control such things. So, I think we can say that the Buddhist position in such debate should, on the one hand, be that of great caution regarding policy and, on the other, great sympathy for those who do resort to it.

No Nature

Question: Can you explain "Buddha Nature"?

Short answer: Buddha nature is no nature.

Longer answer: Buddha nature is no nature. Different writers use the concept in different ways, so to elucidate it one needs to clarify which Buddha nature concept one is referring to. Thus, for instance, there is a common idea that Buddha nature is somehow the core or essence of the person — a kind of soul. This is an idea that has infected Buddhism from time to time, but is not in accord with the principles of non-self, dependent origination and emptiness that are fundamental to the teachings of Shakyamuni. It is more a Hindu or even humanistic psychology idea. A Buddha does not have a fixed nature. A Buddha simply has an absence of malice. However, it has been a problem in the presentation of Buddhism historically that people search for and cling to "positive" forms of expression of the Dharma and this then leads to the coining of many forms of upaya (skilful means). Thus the idea of Buddha nature does not go back to Shakyamuni, but seems to have been invented in the dialectic between Buddhism and other religions. In the West today it is a popular idea because ideas of soul are deeply embedded in Western culture and although people may think they have rejected the theistic ideas, they reinvent them. The soul then becomes the "self-actualising tendency" and so on, and Buddha nature can then be easily saddled onto the same horse. From time to time great teachers — like Nagarjuna — have to come along and dismantle all these constructions. In the meantime, however, if people find them helpful then they are not entirely bad, simply something that will have to be left behind one day.

The idea that there may be something called Buddha nature "within" oneself, therefore, is non-Buddhist. Nagarjuna would no doubt have said that were there any such entity then either it acts or it does not act. If it acts (i.e. if it is the doer of one's "good" deeds, for instance) then it cannot be eternal and must be subject to change, and if it does not act then it has no relevance to life and existence and so is a meaningless idea. Neither way can it really function as one's "true nature". There is no special agent "within" that is responsible for our good and wise actions any more than there is a devil within responsible for our bad and stupid ones. We can loosely and colloquially say that a person is part angel and part devil and so long as we take such expressions lightly and poetically they make sense, but if we try to reify them into a spiritual anatomy of the person we go astray. Buddhism is opposed to that kind of reification in all its varieties.

All this led to a good deal of controversy in Japan in what is called the "critical Buddhism controversy". There is excellent material all about it in the book 'Pruning the Bodhi Tree' by Hubbard & Swanson. There is also a shorter account in my own book 'The New Buddhism'. It is, for instance, sometimes thought that a belief in Buddha nature will make people into better people and insofar as it is simply an expression for seeing the best in others there is much to say for it. However, it has also been pointed out that the deeper logic of the idea that there is an indestructible core of goodness in people leads to the conclusion that it does not matter how badly you treat them because you will never destroy their core anyway, so it does not matter. This idea is strongly developed in the Bhagavad Gita and it is ideas of this kind that Shakyamuni was preaching against. The Critical Buddhists in Japan argue that this line of thinking lies behind many forms of social discrimination in Japanese sectarian Buddhism. We do not need to pursue every detail — sufficient to observe that ideas can be played both ways.

There can also be a kind of subtle arrogance in the idea of thinking that one "has" Buddha nature. It is much safer spiritually to keep one's focus upon one's avidya, upon one's blindness and short-comings. Perhaps I do have a perfect inner nature — so what? Perhaps I have a nature to make mistakes, to hurt people, to be vulnerable — so there is much to do and a basis for fellow-felling with others. If a person really does have a buddha-ly nature then that person is probably not particularly — if at all — aware of it. It might be noticed by others, but even if the person is told so by such an observer, the person in question is likely to say, "Oh, no, no, I'm just an ordinary foolish being."

Thus, in Pureland, the emphasis is upon our bombu nature. This is the root of compassion, modesty and gratitude. It is also the foundation of faith. If one were already of the nature of Buddha, what need would one have of the help of the Buddhas — one would already have everything one needs. It is only when and as I acknowledge my bombu nature that I open myself to the possibility of being helped, of receiving a grace that may lift me out of my karmic plight.

Paradoxically, when I make such an act of humble faith, I do immediately participate in a certain way in the freedom and emptiness of the Tathagatas, since doing so involves letting go of all that I previously had clung to as my nature, and that is how Buddhas are — having no fixed nature, just willing to be whatever is needed, gratefully receiving whatever comes along.

Another slight, yet relevant, tangent to this line of thought is the question of awareness. As just pointed out, the buddha-ly person is not aware of being buddha-like. Saints are generally humble people more conscious of their sins than their virtues. The common idea that spiritual awakening is a function of becoming aware of one's Buddha nature is, therefore, well wide of the mark. To have a buddha-ly nature means to be somebody who acts in the manner of a Buddha quite naturally and when we do things quite naturally we are not especially aware of them. A Buddha is not acutely aware - a Buddha is a natural. Thus Dogen, in Genjokoan, says that enlightened people are not necessarily aware of being so. Certainly, Buddha nature is not a kind of awareness.

For Love

Every community has at its core its discernment of the sacred. Our community has at its heart the nembutsu, which is our expression of our love for the Buddha and, more importantly, our gratitude for his love of us. We gather round the Buddha as the bearer of light: the light of love, the light of compassion, the light of joy, the light of peace, the light that outshines sun, moon and stars, the unimpeded light, light of eternity. Buddhas discern such light, declare it, and walk their talk.

In love of Buddha, therefore, we who are not particularly brave in nature work for peace, for an end to cruelty, for mutual respect, for freedom. In love of Buddha we who are not particularly generous in nature go forth for the good of the many: for the poor in India, for the sick in Africa, for those troubled in spirit in the corners of the affluent world. In love of Buddha we who are not particularly harmonious in nature try to live in goodwill together, making community, and creating the infra-structure of a better world.

We whose ability to discern the light of the world is at best intermittent, nonetheless can remember the love of the awakened ones who are constantly working for the sake of all benighted beings adrift in the flood. In brief, through nembutsu, we resist oppression; through nembutsu we assist the afflicted; through nembutsu we demonstrate an alternative. Our vision is wholly religious, wholly grounded in faith, because we are not enlightened, not perfected, not so wise, not so competent as to be able to do all things by our own power.

Amida Shu has at its core a particular discernment of the sacred, the measureless, the spirit that is the unconditional friend of all, Amida. Amida comes into our lives and transforms our work. We who are bombu are raised up by faith, guided by faith, equalized by faith. The world measures and grades, dividing the legitimate from the illegitimate, the good from the bad, the certificated from the uncertificated. The most that worldly charity offers is access to privilege. Amida transcends such divisions. Before Amida Nyorai we are all equal. In our discernment of the sacred, Amida accepts the bad, the excluded, the uncertificated, the displaced, even more readily than those who are already accomplished or privileged. Nyorai's grace is not limited to those who cultivate the right mind state, pass the right exam, belong to the right lineage, or jump through the right hoops. We are an outpost of Nyorai's Pure Land. We, the misfits, fit here. We are trying to live a life that is genuine — a life free from spin — while recognising that we are just ordinary, unenlightened beings.

Glossary

All words are in English or Sanskrit unless otherwise stated.

adhisthana: spiritual support, power or ground.

akunin: (Japanese) person of 'wrong-doing'. Evil Person.

Ambedkar: (1891-1956) author of the Indian constitution, leader of the untouchables who converted to Buddhism near to the end of his life thereby starting a large scale movement of conversion.

Amida: measureless, the name in the orient of Amitabha or Amitayus Buddha.

Amida Shu: Buddhist church founded by Dharmavidya David Brazier, following Pureland Buddhist teachings.

Amida Sutra: the Smaller Pureland Sutra. A text describing the Pure Land of Sukhavati.

Amidism: a way of describing Amida Shu philosophy and teaching.

Amitabha: Buddha of measureless light.

Ananda: Shakyamuni Buddha's personal attendant during his later years.

anatta: (Pali) not-self, other. Anantma in Sanskrit.

Angulimala: a serial killer and bandit who became a disciple of the Buddha.

anicca: (Pali) impermanence. Anitya in Sanskrit.

anjin: (Japanese) settled faith.

arahant: (Pali) one who is worthy, a Buddhist saint; one who has gained insight into the true nature of existence, overcome greed, hate and delusion, and achieved nirvana; a fully liberated person. Arhat in Sanskrit.

avidya: a-vidya, non-seeing, ignorance, spiritual blindness, inability to see the greater whole or ultimate truth.

bardo: phase in the karmic continuum through many lives, especially the transitional state between death and rebirth.

bodaishin: (Japanese) the mind that desires and moves towards enlightenment. Bodhichitta in Sanskrit.

bodhisattva: a person who has the courage of their enlightened vision, the Buddha before his enlightenment, an angel embodying a particular enlightened quality (bodhisattva of compassion, etc.), a person who has vowed to keep returning to this world lifetime after lifetime in order to help all sentient beings.

bombu: (Japanese) ordinary being of wayward passions, vulnerable, fallible, and imperfect.

Brahma: a heavenly king. Presides over the highest heavenly realm.

brahmin: person belonging to the priestly caste. In the teaching of Shakyamuni, a spiritual person irrespective of caste.

Buddha: can refer to Siddhartha Gotama, the founder of the Buddhist religion or any fully spiritually awakened being.

chi quan: (Chinese) literally 'tranquil mind'. Practice of making offerings to Amida Buddha and receiving the blessing of peace.

Contemplation Sutra: A scripture that tells the story of Queen Vaidehi having a vision of the Pure Land as a result of an encounter with Shakyamuni and goes on to prescribe a visualisation practice approximating her experience.

Dharma: real things, truth, especially spiritual truth, the container of a true life. Probably from a root word meaning to hold, as a mother holds a child. Also the teaching of the Buddha.

Dharmakara: Bodhisattva who became Amida Buddha upon his enlightenment and completion of his 48 vows.

Dharmakaya: Dharma-body. The ultimate nature of Buddha. See: Trikaya.

dhyana: meditation, contemplative absorption, the term from which the Japanese word Zen derives.

dhyanas: particular states of mind or stages which may appear in meditation.

Dogen Zenji: (1200-1253) Japanese Zen master who established Soto Zen in Japan and wrote important works.

dukkha: affliction, situations of spiritual darkness or danger, the first truth for noble ones. Dukka in Pali.

eightfold path: outcome of living a life of faith. Usually taken as instructions for a good life. Right (or wholehearted) view, right thought, right speech, right action, right livelihood, right effort, right mindfulness, right samadhi.

ekagata: independence, singularity, the state of being free from compulsive relationships with internalised others.

four noble truths: more correctly, four truths for noble ones, the first formal teaching given by Shakyamuni. It describes dukkha, its impact and the possibility of redirecting that energy as marga.

guru: teacher.

Hinayana: the smaller vehicle, in contradistinction to Mahayana. Hinayana Buddhism only accepts a canon of scripture written in Pali and adheres to the Arahant ideal rather than that of the bodhisattva. The largest hinayana school today is Theravada, though there are forms of hinayana Buddhism also in East Asia.

Honen Shonin: (1133-1212) Japanese sage who popularised Pureland Buddhism and established the first independent Pureland denomination, Jodo Shu, in Japan.

jiriki: (Japanese) self-power, the belief that one has the power within oneself to achieve spiritual liberation by one's own practice and effort.

Jodo Shin Shu: (Japanese) school of Pureland Buddhism deriving from the teachings of Shinran Shonin, a disciple of Honen Shonin.

Jodo Shu: (Japanese) school of Pureland Buddhism deriving from the teachings of Honen Shonin.

kalpa: an aeon.

karma: drama, intentional action and its consequence.

karuna: a wish that others be freed from affliction. Often translated as compassion.

kensho: (Japanese) a major occurrence of insight or clear seeing, particularly in Zen Buddhism.

klesha: negative mental state; spiritual obstacle.

koan: (Japanese) a universal spiritual barrier occurring in distinctive form in a particular life.

Larger Pureland Sutra: the text which describes Dharmakara becoming Amida Buddha by completing his 48 vows and creating a Pure Land.

lojong: (Tibetan) a purificatory mind training practice.

Lokeshvararaja: The Buddha who inspired Dharmakara to make his 48 vows.

Mahayana: great vehicle, the approach to Buddhism that emphasises the bodhisattva ideal and is found in Tibet, China and across east Asia, in contradistinction to Hinayana. Mahayana schools utilise both Sanskrit and Pali texts, though each school has its favoured works which are usually from the Sanskrit collection.

Maitreya: a Buddha of the future.

maitri: loving kindness.

marga: path, especially the eightfold path (q.v.).

mondo: (Japanese) way of the gate. Ritual question and answer session.

Nagarjuna: Buddhist sage of first century CE who explicated the theory of shunyata and distinguished the difficult (self power) and easy (other power) paths.

Namo Amida Bu: short for Namo Amida Buddha, I take refuge in Amida, a key prayer in oriental spirituality. Has slight variations in different countries, such as Namo Omito Fo in China, Namo Adida Phat in Vietnam etc.

nei quan: (Chinese) investigation inward, meditation upon the evidence of one's life and its dependent nature, related to vipassana.

nembutsu: (Japanese) mental impulse or thought toward Buddha, commonly operationalised as verbal recitation of Buddha's name.

nikaya: (Pali) volume or collection. Usually the Sutta Pitaka — the collection of Buddhist teachings recorded in Pali.

nirmanakaya: Buddha appearing in the world. One of the Trikaya.

nirodha: confinement — the mastery or channelling of the energies that arise in dependence upon dukkha. Complete nirodha is equivalent to nirvana.

nirvana: the extinction of greed, hatred, and delusion.

Nyorai: (Japanese) tathagata — thus come one. An epithet of Buddha.

ojo: (Japanese) rebirth, particularly in Amida's Pure Land.

Om Ami-dewa Hrih: Tibetan form of the mantra of Amitabha (om amitabha hrih), equivalent to nembutsu.

other power: not self power. Originally a term for dependent origination, developed into a term for dependence upon the saving power of Buddhas, designated by Nagarjuna as "the easy path". The belief that one does not have the power within oneself to attain spiritual liberation by one's own efforts, that such liberation comes as a grace

Pali: a language of the Indian sub-continent in which many early Buddhist texts are written.

paramita: other shore, ultimacy, the viewpoint of an enlightened being.

prajna: wisdom.

prasada: clear faith; the realisation of one's own need for refuge.

Pure Land: A realm in which there is a living Buddha.

Pureland Buddhists: Buddhists who follow the teachings of the Pureland Sutras and sages.

Pureland sages: teachers of the Pureland tradition, the most famous being Shan Tao in China and Honen Shonin in Japan.

Quan Shi Yin: (Chinese) the one who hears the cries of the world. A Bodhisattva of compassion.

rinpoche: (Tibetan) precious one. A revered practitioner.

samadhi: consummate vision, concentration, absorption upon a spiritually wholesome objects.

sambhogakaya: the spiritual body of a Buddha. See trikaya.

samjna: trance, entrancement, being hooked by something, ordinary consciousness that skips from one tantalizing or repelling object to another blindly.

samjna-asamjna: an advanced dhyana in which one has objectivity in regard to one's normally entranced mind.

samsara: going round in meaningless circles, the un-free condition of the deluded person.

samskaras: mental formation, attitude, psychological complex. The unnecessary complications that we generate that impede our own lives.

samudaya: co-arising. The spiritual-emotional energy and states of craving that arise in dependence upon the occurrence of dukkha and, in the common case, lead one back into the generation of further dukkha.

Sandokai: (Chinese) an 8th CE. poem recited in Zen temples.

Sangha: the spiritual community, contemporary or ancestral, the spirit of community.

Sanskrit: the classical language of India in which many Buddhist texts were written or recorded. Many of the originally Sanskrit Buddhist texts are now only available in Tibetan and/or Chinese translations.

satori: (Japanese) spiritual awakening that enables one to transcend a koan and enter the spiritual path. Similar to kensho.

self power: reliance upon one's own ability for spiritual salvation. See: jiriki.

senchaku: (Japanese) selection. Honen selected recitation of nembutsu as the essential practice for rebirth in Amida's Pure Land.

Shakyamuni: an epithet of Buddha, sage of the Shakyas.

shamatha: calm meditation, tranquil abiding, stopping in silence and stillness (see also chih quan).

Shan Tao: (613-681) Chinese sage who taught Pureland Buddhism.

shimmitsu: (Japanese) intimacy; a form of faith.

shinjin: awakening of faith.

Shinran: (1173-1263) disciple of Honen Shonin, commonly treated as the founder of the Jodo Shin Shu denomination.

shunya: empty (especially of self).

shunyata: emptiness, especially absence of self-centred distortion, absence of dependence or impermanence.

Siddhartha Gotama: the Buddha.

skandha: aggregate. The five skandha constitute a breakdown of the process by which a mind becomes enslaved by appearance.

Smaller Pureland Sutra: See: Amida Sutra.

sravakas: one who listens, disciple.

stupa: reliquary. A place for remembering and paying reverence to the Buddha or other great saints.

Sukhavati: Joyful-land. Amida's Pure Land.

Tao: (Chinese) way or path.

Taoism: Chinese religion and philosophy of naturalness that uses the yin-yang principle.

tariki: other power (q.v.).

tathagata: as tatha-gata, one who has gone to thusness, a spiritual leader and exemplar; as tatha-agata, one who comes from thusness, a spiritual saviour, friend or helper. See: nyorai.

Theravada: the way of the elders, the form of Buddhism found in south Asia that emphasises the way of the arahant. See: Hinayana.

three jewels: Buddha, Dharma and Sangha.

three Pureland Sutras: the Larger Pureland Sutra, the Amida Sutra and the Contemplation sutra.

tonglen: (Tibetan) a practice where one takes on the suffering of others in order to relieve them.

trikaya: the three bodies or manifestations of a Buddha: absolute (dharmakaya), spiritual (sambhogakaya) and apparent (nirmanakaya).

tulku: (Tibetan) lineage holder who is a reincarnation of a previous teacher.

Udana: (Pali) part of the Pali cannon. The title 'Udana' is often translated as inspired utterances.

upaya: Skilful means.

vinaya: the discipline, or rule, of the monastic community.

vipashyana: (Pali) insight meditation.

yang: (Chinese) sunny-side, bright, masculine. Yin and yang are key principles of Chinese thought, especially in Taoism.

yin: (Chinese) shady-side, dark, feminine. See: yang.

yugen: (Japanese) bitter-sweet. A respected quality in Japanese arts, especially poetry.

Zen: (Japanese) meditation, the name of a denomination of Japanese Buddhism that emphasises meditation practice and sudden awakening.

About David Brazier

David Brazier, Buddhist name, Dharmavidya, has studied and practised in all the major schools of Buddhism and now leads the Amida Sangha, a Pureland Buddhist community. He is an authority on Buddhist psychology and is president of the International Zen Therapy Institute. He is a scholar, doctor of philosophy (PhD), Buddhist priest, author of ten previous books, inspirational lecturer, psychotherapist, social worker, and published poet ("Her Mother's Eyes & Other Poems"). He has founded spiritual communities and aid, education and social work projects in Europe, India and elsewhere as well as training programmes in Buddhist psychology, Zen Therapy and Buddhist ministry. His books include works on psychotherapy, Buddhism and commentary on the relationship between spirituality, art, myth and culture. He has three adult children, five grandchildren, likes gardening, walking and photography and when not travelling remains in retreat in France.

www.ingramcontent.com/pod-product-compliance
Lightning Source LLC
Chambersburg PA
CBHW071155300426
44113CB00009B/1216